THE 1995 NATIONAL JOB HOTLINE DIRECTORY

Marcia P. Williams

Sue A. Cubbage

McGraw-Hill, Inc.

New York   San Francisco   Washington, D.C.   Auckland   Bogotá
Caracas   Lisbon   London   Madrid   Mexico City   Milan
Montreal   New Delhi   San Juan   Singapore
Sydney   Tokyo   Toronto

Library of Congress Cataloging-in-Publication Data

Williams, Marcia P.
   The 1995 national job hotline directory/Marcia P. Williams, Sue A. Cubbage
      p.   cm.
   ISBN 0-07-070593-3 (pbk.)
   1. Job hotlines—United States—Directories. 2. Job vacancies—United States—Telephone directories. 3. Business enterprises—United States—Telephone directories. 4. Civil service positions—United States—Telephone directories. I. Cubbage, Sue A. II. Title.
HF5382.75.U6W53   1994
331.12'8'02573—dc20
                                                                                       94-5477
                                                                                            CIP

Copyright © 1994 by McGraw-Hill, Inc. All rights reserved. Printed in the United States of America. Except as permitted under the United States Copyright Act of 1976, no part of this publication may be reproduced or distributed in any form or by any means, or stored in a data base or retrieval system, without the prior written permission of the publisher.

1 2 3 4 5 6 7 8 9 0   DOC/DOC   9 0 9 8 7 6 5 4

ISBN 0-07-070593-3

The sponsoring editor for this book was Betsy N. Brown, the editing supervisor was Joseph Bertuna, and the production supervisor was Pamela A. Pelton. It was set in Goudy by McGraw-Hill's Professional Book Group composition unit.

Printed and bound by R. R. Donnelley & Sons Company.

This book is printed on recycled, acid-free paper containing a minimum of 50% recycled, de-inked fiber.

*This book is dedicated to the memory
of
Julie M. Reimers
(1927–1993)*

Contents

Acknowledgments   vii
Preface   ix
Area Codes   xi

STATE LISTINGS

Alabama   3
Alaska   8
Arizona   12
Arkansas   25
California   26
Colorado   69
Connecticut   89
Delaware   91
District of Columbia   93
Florida   101
Georgia   115
Hawaii   127
Idaho   130
Illinois   133
Indiana   137
Iowa   142
Kansas   144
Kentucky   147
Louisiana   150
Maine   152
Maryland   153
Massachusetts   160
Michigan   162
Minnesota   164
Mississippi   166
Missouri   168

Montana   174
Nebraska   178
Nevada   182
New Hampshire   185
New Jersey   187
New Mexico   189
New York   191
North Carolina   195
North Dakota   199
Ohio   201
Oklahoma   205
Oregon   210
Pennsylvania   221
Rhode Island   223
South Carolina   224
South Dakota   227
Tennessee   228
Texas   233
Utah   256
Vermont   261
Virginia   262
Washington   274
West Virginia   289
Wisconsin   290
Wyoming   293

OTHER LISTINGS

National Joblines   *297*
International Listings   *302*
Mail Joblines   *304*

Reply Form   *306*

Acknowledgments

The 1995 National Job Hotline Directory is my dream. I see it as a way of providing necessary information and assistance to people who are out of work, changing careers, or relocating.

When I started, I had no idea of the size of the project in which I was getting involved. From obtaining a publisher, to doing the actual research and organization, it has been more than one person could handle. Accordingly, I would like to acknowledge the following people who have made this book possible.

My parents, Charles and Barbara Williams, provided much-needed technical assistance. Dr. L. Pearce Williams was instrumental in presenting the idea to McGraw-Hill and guiding me through the publication process. Sue Cubbage did most of the organization and verification work and earned her place as my coauthor.

Since I have worked a full-time job at the State of Colorado, Department of Labor and Employment, while compiling the material, I want to acknowledge the assistance and support of coworkers, Cindy Haugen, Joyce Martinez, Greg Carson, Tara Singh, Pam White, John Barton, Terry Steffey, Larry Beasley, Betty Adams, and Audrey Rodriguez.

A special salute is due to Ginnie Weiner, manager of the North Metro Job Service Center, Westminster, Colorado, who has been a friend, mentor, and role model.

I would also like to acknowledge the following people, who believed in my idea and gave me much encouragement, JoAnn Richter, John Klube, Pam Staples, Sharon Harlow, and Joanne Jorgenson.

Additionally, many thanks to Sue Cubbage's mother, Lucille (Lucy) Cubbage, and friend Jacque Chambers, who traveled hither and yon in search of telephone directories, oftentimes having no idea where they were, let alone where they were going.

Finally, I would like to thank my roommate, Connie Romano, who tolerated me during all of this but never quite got used to my reading telephone directories.

Marcia P. Williams

Preface

Thank you for choosing *The 1995 National Job Hotline Directory* as part of your job search. If you are not exactly sure what a job hotline is or how the directory can best serve your needs, please read on.

A job hotline is, typically, a taped recording of job vacancies that can be accessed by dialing a telephone number. They can be found in almost any area of employment. Government agencies, as well as private industry, use joblines as an effective way of recruiting personnel and cutting costs.

The 1995 National Job Hotline Directory is organized alphabetically by state, and also contains some national, international, and mail joblines. Within each state, joblines are further broken down into the following categories: Cities, Counties, State, Federal, Banks, Education, Hotels, Medical/Hospitals, and Miscellaneous employers.

To make the most of the directory, and your time, we suggest you follow these steps:

- Take time to review the entire book, and get a feel for the information it will provide. Give consideration to your criteria. For example, is location of most importance, or is what you do (and for whom you work) the major concern? Once you have determined this, you can effectively use the directory.

- Most joblines require the use of a touch-tone telephone. If you have a rotary telephone, you *may not* be able to access the jobline and will have to wait for an operator or the personnel office to answer. Additionally, you may have to place your call during normal business hours. When equipment for the hearing impaired is available, we have noted this with the abbreviations TDD or TTY.

- Except where noted, joblines can be accessed 24 hours a day, thus allowing you to call the line during low-telephone-rate periods, as most joblines *are not* toll-free.
- Joblines are usually updated every week or every other week, normally on Monday or Friday.
- Some 800-numbers are accessible nationwide while some are accessible only within that particular state. We have tried to note this where possible. When there are two numbers for the same place, and one is an 800-number, it means that it is for people from out of the area (out of state) to use toll free.
- Have a pen and paper handy to take down the necessary information, in the event you find a position in which you are interested.

The 1995 National Job Hotline Directory is not a guarantee of a job, but it is an important tool to assist you in your job search. It will allow you to do more of your search from home, using a telephone, regardless of whether you are searching locally or seeking to relocate.

This is a unique publication containing approximately 3500 entries. All possible efforts have been taken to ensure that it is user-friendly and correct. Unfortunately, we cannot guarantee that all numbers will be in service or unchanged due to the ever-changing needs of the organizations listed. Also, please note that many entry locations are given as the closest major city to allow the user to better identify a general area.

We welcome your comments and suggestions, corrections, and additions to be considered for future publications. Please use the page at the end of the book for that purpose.

Finally, we hope that you will find this resource valuable in your job search and wish you much success.

Marcia P. Williams
Sue A. Cubbage

Area Codes

Alabama......................................205
  Birmingham
  *Montgomery

Alaska 907
  Anchorage
  *Juneau

Arizona 602
  *Phoenix
  Tucson

Arkansas 501
  *Little Rock

California
  Anaheim 714
  Bakersfield.............................805
  Fresno....................................209
  Los Angeles....................213/310
  Oakland 510
  Pasadena 818
  *Sacramento 916
  San Bernardino 909
  San Diego..............................619
  San Francisco.........................415
  San Jose.................................408
  Santa Rosa 707

Colorado
  Boulder..................................303
  Colorado Springs 719
  *Denver 303

  Fort Collins 303
  Grand Junction 303
  Pueblo 719

Connecticut...............................203
  *Hartford

Delaware 302
  *Dover
  Wilmington

District of Columbia 202

Florida
  Fort Lauderdale 305
  Jacksonville...........................904
  Miami...................................305
  Orlando................................407
  *Tallahasse 904
  Tampa 813

Georgia
  *Atlanta.................................404
  Augusta 706
  Savannah 912

Hawaii.......................................808
  *Honolulu
  Islands:
    Hawaii
    Lanai
    Maui
    Molokai
    Oahu (Honolulu)

xi

Idaho............208
  *Boise
  Idaho Falls
  Pocatello

Illinois
  Alton.....................618
  Carbondale............618
  Chicago................312 (City)
  Chicago................708 (Suburbs)
  Peoria...................309
  Rockford...............815
  *Springfield...........217

Indiana
  Evansville..............812
  Gary......................219
  *Indianapolis........317

Iowa
  Council Bluffs.......712
  *Des Moines.........515
  Dubuque...............319

Kansas
  Dodge City............316
  Hutchinson...........316
  Kansas City...........913
  Lawrence...............913
  Manhattan.............913
  Overland Park.......913
  *Topeka.................913
  Wichita..................316

Kentucky
  Covington..............606
  *Frankfort..............502
  Lexington...............606
  Louisville...............502

Louisiana
  *Baton Rouge.........504
  Lake Charles..........318
  New Orleans..........504

Maine............207
  *Augusta
  Bangor
  Portsmouth

Maryland
  *Annapolis............301
  Baltimore..............410
  Silver Springs........301

Massachusetts
  *Boston.................617
  Springfield.............413
  Worcester..............508

Michigan
  Ann Arbor.............313
  Detroit..................313
  Grand Rapids........616
  *Lansing................517
  Marquette..............906

Minnesota
  Duluth..................218
  Minneapolis..........612
  Rochester..............507
  *St. Paul................612

Mississippi............601
  *Jackson

Missouri
  *Jefferson City......314
  Kansas City..........816
  St. Louis...............314
  Springfield............417

Area Codes

Montana 406
 *Helena

Nebraska
 *Lincoln....................................402
 North Platte............................308
 Omaha 402

Nevada.......................................702
 *Carson City
 Las Vegas
 Reno

New Hampshire 603
 *Concord

New Jersey
 Atlantic City 609
 Camden..................................609
 Newark...................................201
 New Brunswick......................908
 *Trenton..................................609

New Mexico...............................505
 Albuquerque
 *Santa Fe

New York
 *Albany 518
 Binghamton 607
 Buffalo....................................716
 Long Island 516
 Manhattan 212
 New York City................212/718
 Queens 718
 Rochester 716
 Syracuse 315
 White Plains 914

North Carolina
 Charlotte................................704

*Raleigh....................................919

North Dakota............................701
 *Bismarck
 Fargo
 Grand Forks

Ohio
 Akron.....................................216
 Cincinnati..............................513
 Cleveland...............................216
 *Columbus..............................614
 Dayton 513
 Toledo....................................419

Oklahoma
 Enid..405
 Lawton 405
 Norman..................................405
 *Oklahoma City 405
 Stillwater................................405
 Tulsa 918

Oregon 503
 *Salem

Pennsylvania
 Erie...814
 *Harrisburg 717
 Philadelphia...........................215
 Pittsburgh...............................412

Rhode Island.............................401
 *Providence

South Carolina 803
 *Columbia

South Dakota............................605
 *Pierre

Tennessee
  Knoxville 615
  Memphis 901
  *Nashville................................615

Texas
  Abilene 915
  Amarillo..................................806
  *Austin 512
  Beaumont................................409
  Corpus Christi 512
  Dallas 214
  El Paso....................................915
  Fort Worth..............................817
  Galveston................................409
  Houston 713
  Lubbock..................................806
  San Antonio 210
  Tyler..903
  Wichita Falls...........................817

Utah...801
  *Salt Lake City

Vermont......................................802
  *Montpelier

Virginia
  Arlington 703
  Norfolk....................................804
  *Richmond 804

Washington
  *Olympia 206
  Seattle 206
  Spokane 509
  Vancouver...............................206

West Virginia..............................304
  *Charleston

Wisconsin
  Eau Claire 715
  *Madison 608
  Milwaukee...............................414

Wyoming 307
  *Cheyenne

Other Area Codes

Canada
  Ottawa 613
  British Columbia....................604
  Ontario
    London................................519
    North Bay 705

Puerto Rico 809

Virgin Islands.............................809

* Denotes State Capitol.

State Listings

Alabama

Cities

Dothan
 (205) 793-0309

Hunstville
 (205) 535-4942

Huntsville
 (205) 532-4746 (May contain same information as previous entry)

Montgomery (City and County)
 (205) 241-2217

Counties

Madison (Huntsville)
 (205) 532-6906

Federal

United States Postal Service (Huntsville)
 (205) 461-6646

United States Postal Service (Montgomery)
 (205) 244-7551

Banks

First Alabama Bank (Huntsville)
 (205) 326-7434

First Alabama Bank (Mobile)
(205) 690-1306

Central Bank of the South (Huntsville)
(205) 532-6330

Secor Bank (Birmingham)
(205) 877-0504

Education

Auburn University (Birmingham)
(205) 844-4336

Auburn University (Montgomery)
(205) 244-3218

Huntsville City Schools (Huntsville)
(205) 532-4746

Samford University (Birmingham)
(205) 870-2103

University of Alabama (Birmingham)
(205) 934-2611

University of Alabama (Huntsville)
(205) 895-6105

University of Alabama (Tuscaloosa)
(205) 348-7780

Hotels

Sheraton Civic Center Hotel (Birmingham)
(205) 307-3016

Medical/Hospitals

AMI Brookwood Medical Center (Birmingham)
(205) 877-1910

Alabama

Blue Cross/Blue Shield of Alabama (Birmingham)
(205) 988-2554

Children's Hospital (Birmingham)
(205) 939-9188

DCH Regional Medical Center (Tuscaloosa)
(205) 759-7911

Eye Foundation Hospital (Birmingham)
(205) 325-8589

Health South Medical Center (South Birmingham)
(205) 933-2252

Humana Hospital (East Montgomery)
(205) 244-8583

Huntsville Hospital (Huntsville)
(205) 533-8225

Lakeshore Rehabilitation Hospital (Birmingham)
(205) 868-2307

Lloyd Noland Health System (Birmingham)
(205) 783-8805

Medical Center East (Birmingham)
(205) 802-8518

Medical Center Hospital (Huntsville)
(205) 532-5855

Montclair Baptist Medical Center (Birmingham)
(205) 868-9900

Princeton Baptist Medical Center (Birmingham)
(205) 868-9900   Category 6846

Providence Hospital (Mobile)
(205) 633-1099

Roche Biomedical Laboratories Incorporated
  (Birmingham)
  (205) 581-3655

St. Vincent Hospital (Birmingham)
  (205) 939-7298

Southeast Alabama Medical Center (Tuscaloosa)
  (205) 793-8000

Springhill Memorial Hospital (Mobile)
  (205) 460-5296

Miscellaneous

Alabama Gas Corporation (Birmingham)
  (205) 326-8190

Alabama Power Company (Birmingham)
  (205) 250-2612

American Cast Iron Pipe Company (Birmingham)
  (205) 325-8010

American Telephone & Telegraph (Statewide)
  (800) 562-7288

American Telephone & Telegraph (Statewide)
  (800) 562-7665 (TDD)

Bell South Cellular (Statewide)
  (800) 669-0136

Birmingham News (Birmingham)
  (205) 325-2188

Colsa Corporation (Birmingham)
  (205) 922-1512   Ext. 4000

EBSCO Industries Incorporated (Birmingham)
  (205) 991-1477

Alabama

Protective Life Insurance Company (Birmingham)
(205) 868-3125

Southern Company Services Incorporated (Homewood)
(205) 870-6799

Southern Living (Birmingham)
(205) 877-6199

Southern Natural Gas Company (Birmingham)
(205) 325-7263

Southern Progress (Birmingham)
(205) 877-6199

South Trust Mortgage Corporation (Huntsville)
(205) 721-7163

Vulcan Materials Company (Birmingham)
(205) 877-3986

Alaska

Cities

Anchorage
 (907) 343-4451

Counties

Fairbanks/North Star Borough
 (907) 459-1209

State

Alaska Employment Service (Anchorage)
 (907) 269-4730 (Crafts and Trades)

Alaska Employment Service (Anchorage)
 (907) 269-4735 (Part Time)

Alaska Employment Service (Anchorage)
 (907) 269-4740 (Professional/Technical/Clerical)

Alaska Employment Service (Anchorage)
 (907) 269-4725 (Sales and Service)

Alaska Employment Service (Anchorage)
 (907) 269-4765 (Seafood)

Alaska Employment Service (Anchorage)
 (907) 269-4750 (Youth)

Alaska Employment Service (Fairbanks)
 (907) 451-2875

Alaska Employment Service (Juneau)
(907) 790-4571

Federal

Federal Job Information Line (Anchorage)
(907) 271-5821

Fort Richardson (Anchorage)
(907) 384-1376

Fort Wainwright (North Pole)
(907) 353-7200

Banks

Bank of America (Anchorage)
(907) 263-3206

First National Bank of Anchorage (Anchorage)
(907) 265-3027

Key Bank of Alaska (Anchorage)
(907) 257-5583

National Bank of Alaska (Anchorage)
(907) 257-3299

Education

Fairbanks/North Star Borough School District
(Fairbanks)
(907) 456-8077

University of Alaska (Anchorage)
(907) 786-4887

Hotels

Anchorage Hilton (Anchorage)
 (907) 265-7124

Medical/Hospitals

Alaska Regional Hospital (Anchorage)
 (907) 264-1539

Blue Cross/Blue Shield (Statewide)
 (206) 670-4773

Providence Hospital (Anchorage)
 (907) 261-3049

Miscellaneous

ALASCOM (Anchorage)
 (907) 264-7112

Alaska Airlines (Statewide)
 (206) 433-3230

Alaska Children's Service Center (Anchorage)
 (907) 346-1271

Alaska Railroad (Anchorage)
 (907) 265-2430

Alyeska Pipeline (Statewide)
 (907) 265-8980

Anchorage Daily News (Anchorage)
 (907) 257-4402

Anchorage Telephone (Anchorage)
 (907) 564-1515

ARCO Alaska (Anchorage)
 (907) 263-4100

Alaska

B. P. Exploration (Anchorage/North Star)
(907) 564-4999

Enstar Natural Gas (Anchorage)
(907) 264-3688

ERA Aviation (Anchorage)
(907) 266-8346

GCI (Anchorage)
(907) 275-3038

Hope Cottages (Anchorage)
(907) 564-7484

Landmark Group (Anchorage)
(907) 275-3387

MarkAir (Anchorage)
(907) 266-6731

Mila Corporation (Anchorage)
(907) 562-1822

Northwest Library Association (Statewide)
(206) 543-2890

Piquniq Management Corporation (Anchorage)
(907) 267-2743

South Central Counseling Center (Anchorage)
(907) 249-9260

Arizona

Cities

Apache Junction
 (602) 982-8002 (Press 6, Then 1)

Chandler
 (602) 786-2294

Gilbert
 (602) 497-4950

Glendale
 (602) 435-4402

Mesa
 (602) 644-2759

Peoria
 (602) 412-7105

Phoenix
 (602) 252-5627 (General)

Phoenix
 (602) 262-7356 (Police/Fire)

Scottsdale
 (602) 994-2395

Tempe
 (602) 350-8217

Tucson
 (602) 791-5068

Arizona

Tucson
 (602) 791-2639 (TDD)

Counties

Maricopa (Phoenix)
 (602) 506-3329 (General)

Maricopa (Phoenix)
 (602) 681-8080 (Health Services)

Maricopa (Phoenix)
 (602) 506-1908 (TDD)

Pima (Tucson)
 (602) 740-3530

Pinal (Florence)
 (602) 868-6599

State

Arizona Department of Public Safety (Statewide)
 (602) 223-2148

Arizona State Jobline (Phoenix)
 (602) 542-4966

Arizona State Jobline (Tucson)
 (602) 792-2853

Federal

Federal Job Information Center (Phoenix)
 (602) 640-4800

Luke Air Force Base (Litchfield Park)
 (602) 856-7745

Resolution Trust Corporation (Phoenix)
 (602) 224-1778

United States Postal Service (Phoenix)
(602) 225-3189

United States Postal Service (Statewide)
(602) 223-3624

Banks

Bank of America (Phoenix)
(602) 594-2500

Bank One of Arizona (Phoenix)
(602) 221-2441

Bank One Mortgage Company (Phoenix)
(602) 221-7899

Caliber Bank (Phoenix)
(602) 640-4450

Chase Bank (Phoenix)
(602) 902-6000

Citibank (Tucson)
(602) 620-3660

Citibank of Arizona (Phoenix)
(602) 248-1283

First Interstate Bank of Arizona (Phoenix)
(602) 528-1199

Education

Alhambra School District (Alhambra)
(602) 246-5128

Amuhi School District (Phoenix)
(602) 292-4221

Arizona

Arizona State University (Tempe)
(602) 965-JOBS

Arizona State University West (Phoenix)
(602) 543-JOBS

Cartwright School District No. 83 (Phoenix)
(602) 846-2800   Ext. 5

Catalina School District (Tucson)
(602) 577-5310

Catalina School District (Tucson)
(602) 299-6446 (Rotary Telephones)

Chandler-Gilbert Community College (Phoenix)
(602) 731-8444

Chandler Public Schools (Phoenix)
(602) 786-7016

Deer Valley Unified School District (Deer Valley)
(602) 581-7748

Dysart Unified School District (Dysart)
(602) 965-0506

Flagstaff Public Schools (Flagstaff)
(602) 527-6080

Flowing Wells Schools (Flowing Wells)
(602) 888-3172

Glendale Elementary School District No. 40 (Glendale)
(602) 842-8170

Grand Canyon University (Phoenix)
(602) 589-2407

Kyrene Elementary School District (Phoenix)
(602) 496-4773 (Certified)

Kyrene Elementary School District (Phoenix)
(602) 496-4674 (Classified)

Madison School District (Phoenix)
(602) 277-2058

Marana Public Schools (Phoenix)
(602) 798-1122

Maricopa Community College (Phoenix)
(602) 731-8444

Mesa Public Schools (Mesa)
(602) 890-7028

Northern Arizona University (Flagstaff)
(602) 523-5627

Paradise Valley Unified School District (Phoenix)
(602) 867-5224

Peoria Unified School District No. 11 (Peoria)
(602) 486-6190

Phoenix Elementary School District No. 1 (Phoenix)
(602) 257-3611

Phoenix Union High School District (Phoenix)
(602) 271-3111

Pima Community College (Tucson)
(602) 884-6623

Roosevelt School District (Phoenix)
(602) 276-4326

School for the Deaf and Blind (Tucson)
(602) 628-6026

School for the Deaf and Blind (Tucson)
(602) 770-3712 (May contain same information as previous entry)

Arizona

Scottsdale Unified School District (Scottsdale)
(602) 952-6296

Sunnyside Unified School District (Tucson)
(602) 741-2546

Tempe Elementary Schools (Tempe)
(602) 839-7114

Tempe Union High School District (Tempe)
(602) 820-0461

Tucson Unified School District No. 1 (Tucson)
(602) 882-1516

University of Arizona (Tucson)
(602) 621-3087 (English)

University of Arizona (Tucson)
(602) 621-5237 (Spanish)

University of Phoenix (Phoenix)
(602) 929-7359

Washington Elementary School District (Phoenix)
(602) 864-2689

Hotels

Arizona Biltmore Resort (Phoenix)
(602) 954-2547

Canyon Ranch (Tucson)
(602) 749-9655

El Conquistador Resort (Tucson)
(602) 544-1240

Pointe Hilton Resort (Phoenix)
(602) 438-9303

Princess Resort (Scottsdale)
 (602) 585-2755

The Wigwam Resort (Phoenix)
 (602) 856-1048

Medical/Hospitals

Arizona State Hospital (Phoenix)
 (602) 542-4966

Arrowhead Community Hospital (Phoenix)
 (602) 561-7200

Blue Cross/Blue Shield of Arizona (Phoenix)
 (602) 864-4339

Blue Cross/Blue Shield of Arizona (Phoenix)
 (602) 864-5455 (TDD)

Boswell Memorial Hospital (Phoenix)
 (602) 974-7894

Carondolet Health Care (Tucson)
 (602) 721-3874

Chandler Regional Hospital (Phoenix)
 (602) 821-3113   Ext. 4

CIGNA Health Plan of Arizona (Phoenix)
 (602) 942-4462

CIGNA Health Plan of Arizona (Tucson)
 (602) 571-6655

Desert Samaritan Medical Center (Phoenix)
 (602) 835-3180   Ext. 5082

FHP Healthcare (Phoenix)
 (602) 244-8200   Ext. 4

Arizona

Flagstaff Medical Center (Flagstaff)
(602) 773-2067

GHMA Medical Center (Tucson)
(602) 721-3519

Healthwest Regional Medical Center (Phoenix)
(602) 241-7635

John C. Lincoln Hospital (Phoenix)
(602) 870-6360

Lincoln Health Center (Phoenix)
(602) 870-6369 (Nursing)

Lincoln Health Center (Phoenix)
(602) 870-6329 (Nonnursing)

Maricopa Medical Center (Phoenix)
(602) 681-8080

Mesa General Hospital (Phoenix)
(602) 844-4199

Mesa Lutheran Hospital (Phoenix)
(602) 461-2562

Phoenix Baptist Hospital and Medical Center
(Phoenix)
(602) 246-5627

Phoenix Children's Hospital (Phoenix)
(602) 239-4466

Phoenix General Hospital and Medical Center
(Phoenix)
(602) 879-5660

Phoenix Memorial Hospital (Phoenix)
(602) 238-3573

Phoenix South Community Mental Health Center
(Phoenix)
(602) 468-7345

Planned Parenthood (Phoenix)
(602) 227-7722   Ext. 5

St. Joseph's Hospital and Medical Center (Phoenix)
(Available 8 A.M. to 5 P.M.; ask for Jobline)

St. Joseph's Hospital and Medical Center (Phoenix)
(602) 285-3035 (Allied Health)

St. Joseph's Hospital and Medical Center (Phoenix)
(800) 662-JOBS (Allied Health)

St. Joseph's Hospital and Medical Center (Phoenix)
(602) 285-3118 (Nursing)

St. Joseph's Hospital and Medical Center (Phoenix)
(800) SJ3-NURS (Nursing)

Scottsdale Memorial Hospital System (Scottsdale)
(602) 941-5221

Southern Arizona Rehabilitation Hospital (Tucson)
(602) 544-5214

Sun Health Corporation (Phoenix)
(602) 974-7984

Tempe Center for Habilitation (Tempe)
(602) 894-2704

Tucson General Hospital (Tucson)
(602) 323-4334

Tucson Medical Center (Tucson)
(602) 324-2600

University Physicians (Tucson)
(602) 322-6080

Arizona

Valley Lutheran Hospital (Mesa)
(602) 461-2562

Webb Memorial Hospital (Phoenix)
(602) 974-7984

Miscellaneous

America West Airlines (Phoenix)
(602) 693-8650

American Express (West Region Operation Center)
(602) 492-5627

American Telephone & Telegraph (Phoenix)
(602) 233-5169

Arizona Library Association (Statewide)
(602) 275-2325

Arizona Public Service Company (Phoenix)
(602) 250-3369

Arizona Republic (Phoenix)
(602) 238-4445

Artisoft Incorporated (Tucson)
(602) 670-4201

Avis (Phoenix)
(602) 273-3209

Basha's (Phoenix)
(602) 895-5300

Bull HN Worldwide Information Systems (Phoenix)
(602) 862-5785

Burr-Brown Corporation (Tucson)
(602) 746-7740

Coca-Cola Bottling Company (Phoenix)
(602) 831-0400   Ext. 3322

Dial Corporation (Phoenix)
(602) 207-5787

Discover Card (Phoenix)
(602) 481-2460

First Data Corporation (Tucson)
(602) 795-8838

Fleming Foods (Phoenix)
(602) 269-5244

Garrett Airline Service (Chandler)
(602) 731-5103

GFC Financial Corporation (Phoenix)
(602) 207-6905

Holsum Bakery (Phoenix)
(602) 229-8137

Honeywell Space and Aviation Systems (Phoenix)
(602) 436-2027

Hughes Aircraft (Tucson)
(602) 794-8484

Intel Corporation (Phoenix)
(602) 554-5726

International Business Machines (Phoenix)
(602) 224-2700

International Business Machines (Tucson)
(602) 799-2300

KPNX (Phoenix)
(602) 257-1212

La Frontera Center Incorporated (Tucson)
(602) 770-7406

Arizona

La Frontera Center Incorporated (Tucson)
(602) 844-9920 (TDD)

Learjet Incorporated (Tucson)
(602) 746-5370

McDonnell Douglas Helicopter Company (Mesa)
(602) 891-3100

Medtronic Micro-Rel (Phoenix)
(602) 929-5444

Mesa Tribune (Phoenix)
(602) 898-5600

Microage (Phoenix)
(602) 968-3168   Ext. 0 (Ask for Jobline, 8 A.M. to
5 P.M., Mon. through Fri., Mountain Time)

Motorola Incorporated–Goverment Electronics Group
(Phoenix)
(602) 441-3425

Motorola Semi-Conductor Products Sector (Tempe)
(602) 994-6811

Mountain Plains Library Association (Statewide)
(605) 677-5757

Mountain Plains Library Association (Statewide)
(800) 356-7820 (Within state only)

Orbital Sciences Corporation (Phoenix)
(602) 814-6580

Phoenix America West Arena (Phoenix)
(602) 379-2088

Phoenix Transit (Phoenix)
(602) 262-7191

Pizza Hut (Phoenix)
(602) 244-4437

Salt River Project (Tempe)
(602) 236-8374

Smith's Food and Drug (Phoenix)
(602) 936-2400

Southwest Airlines (Phoenix)
(602) 389-3738

Southwest Gas Corporation (Phoenix)
(602) 861-0664

Southwest Gas Corporation (Tucson)
(602) 794-6537

Tucson Airport Authority (Tucson)
(602) 573-8154

Tucson Electric and Power Company (Tucson)
(602) 884-3618

Valley Temporary Services (Phoenix)
(602) 548-1153

W. L. Gore and Associates Incorporated (Flagstaff)
(602) 526-6881

Arkansas

Cities

Little Rock
 (501) 371-4505

Federal

Little Rock Air Force Base (Little Rock)
 (501) 988-8189

Education

University of Arkansas (Fayetteville)
 (501) 575-JOBS

Medical/Hospitals

HCA Doctors Hospital (Little Rock)
 (501) 661-4467

Rebsamen Regional Medical Center (Jacksonville)
 (501) 985-7043

St. Vincent Infirmary Medical Center (Little Rock)
 (501) 660-3430 (Nursing)

St. Vincent Infirmary Medical Center (Little Rock)
 (501) 660-3167 (Nonnursing)

California

Cities

Alameda
(510) 748-4635

Albany
(415) 528-5777   Ext. 714

Alhambra
(818) 570-3295

Anaheim
(714) 254-5197

Antioch
(510) 778-0385

Bakersfield
(805) 326-3773

Baldwin Park
(818) 813-5206

Benica
(707) 745-1371

Berkeley
(510) 644-6122

Brea
(714) 671-4420

Burbank
(818) 953-9724

California

Carmel-by-the-Sea
(408) 624-7045

Chino
(909) 391-9808

Chula Vista
(619) 691-5095

Clovis
(209) 297-2329

Concord
(510) 671-3151

Coronado City
(619) 522-7807

Costa Mesa
(714) 754-5070

Covina
(818) 858-7225

Daly City
(415) 991-8029

Davis
(916) 757-5645

El Cajon
(619) 441-1671

Eureka
(707) 443-8477

Fairfield
(707) 428-7396

Fountain Valley
(714) 965-4409

Fremont
(510) 745-8901

Fresno
(209) 498-1573

Fullerton
(714) 738-6378

Garden Grove
(714) 741-5016

Hayward
(510) 293-5313

Huntington Beach
(714) 374-1570

Irvine
(714) 724-6096

La Mesa
(619) 462-1540   Ext. 183

Long Beach
(310) 590-6201

Los Angeles
(213) 485-2441

Milpitas
(408) 262-5146

Modesto
(209) 577-5498

Montebello
(213) 887-1380

Monterey
(408) 646-3751

California

Mountain View
 (415) 903-6310

Napa
 (707) 257-9542

National City
 (619) 336-4306

Newark
 (510) 745-1184

Oakland
 (510) 238-3111

Ontario
 (909) 391-2580

Orange
 (714) 966-4025 (Department of Education)

Orange
 (714) 744-7262 (General)

Oxnard
 (805) 385-7580

Palo Alto
 (415) 329-2222

Pasadena
 (818) 405-4600

Pico Rivera
 (818) 801-4387

Pismo Beach
 (805) 773-7065

Pleasant Hill
 (510) 671-5255

Riverside
 (909) 782-5492

Sacramento
 (916) 443-9990 (General)

Sacramento
 (916) 440-1336 (Housing and Redevelopment Agency)

San Bernardino
 (909) 387-5611

San Diego
 (619) 450-6210 (General)

San Diego
 (619) 236-6463 (General—may contain same information as previous entry)

San Diego
 (619) 291-0110 (Port of San Diego)

San Francisco
 (415) 557-4888 (City and County)

San Francisco
 (415) 206-5317 (Public Housing)

San Francisco
 (415) 554-1669 (Public Utilities)

San Jose
 (408) 277-5627

San Leandro
 (510) 577-3397

San Mateo
 (415) 377-3359

San Palo
 (415) 329-2222

California

San Ramon
(510) 275-2338

Santa Ana
(714) 953-9675

Santa Clara
(408) 984-3150

Santa Cruz
(408) 429-3040

Santa Monica
(310) 458-8697

Santa Rosa
(707) 524-5823

Santee
(619) 258-4123

Seaside
(408) 899-6255

South San Francisco
(415) 877-3976

Stockton
(209) 944-8523

Torrance
(310) 618-2969

Vallejo
(707) 648-4364

Ventura
(805) 658-4777

Victorville
(619) 245-7499

Walnut Creek
(510) 943-5817

West Covina
(818) 814-8452

West Hollywood
(310) 854-7309

West Sacramento
(916) 371-5669

Whittier
(818) 945-8226

Woodland
(916) 661-5810

Yuba City
(916) 741-4766

Counties

Alameda (Alameda)
(510) 272-6433

Contra Costa (Martinez)
(510) 646-4046   Ext. 2

El Dorado (Placerville)
(916) 621-5579

Monterey (Monterey)
(408) 755-5126

Nevada (Nevada City)
(916) 265-1366

Orange (Santa Ana)
(714) 834-5627

Placer (Auburn)
(916) 889-4070

Riverside (Riverside)
(909) 275-3550

California

Sacramento (Sacramento)
(916) 440-6771 (General)

Sacramento (Sacramento)
(916) 366-4302 (Office of Education)

San Bernardino (San Bernardino)
(909) 387-5611

San Diego (San Diego)
(619) 531-5764 (General)

San Diego (San Diego)
(619) 974-2013 (Sheriff's Department)

San Joaquin (Stockton)
(209) 468-3377

San Mateo (San Mateo)
(415) 368-7214

Santa Clara (Santa Clara)
(408) 453-6926 (County Office of Education)

Santa Clara (Santa Clara)
(408) 299-2856 (General)

Santa Cruz (Santa Cruz)
(408) 425-2377

Solano (Fairfield)
(707) 421-6740

Sonoma (Santa Rosa)
(707) 527-2803

Stanislaus (Modesto)
(209) 525-4339

Sutter (Yuba City)
(916) 671-1687

Yolo (Woodland)
(916) 666-8159

State

State of California (Statewide)
(800) 727-JOBS (Department of Corrections)

State of California (Statewide)
(916) 227-2117 (Department of Corrections)

State of California (Los Angeles)
(213) 897-3154

State of California (Sacramento)
(916) 369-3624 (Franchise Tax Board)

State of California (Sacramento)
(916) 445-0538 (General)

State of California (Sacramento)
(916) 322-0023 (State Lottery)

State of California (San Diego)
(619) 237-6163

State of California (San Francisco)
(415) 557-7871

Federal

Ames Research Center (San Francisco)
(415) 604-8000

Beale Air Force Base (Marysville)
(916) 634-4375

Bureau of Reclamation (Sacramento)
(916) 978-4897

Central Intelligence Agency (Pasadena)
(818) 442-4845

Federal Job Information Center (Sacramento)
(916) 551-1464

California

Federal Job Information Center (San Diego)
(619) 557-6165

Federal Job Information Center (San Francisco)
(415) 744-5627

Federal Reserve Bank of San Francisco (San Francisco)
(415) 974-3330

Fort Irwin (Fort Irwin)
(619) 386-3305

Golden Gate National Recreation Area (San Francisco)
(415) 556-1839

McClellan Air Force Base (Sacramento)
(916) 643-5911

Naval Department of Public Works Center (San Diego)
(619) 556-2490

North Island Naval Air Station (San Diego)
(619) 545-1620

United States Geological Survey (San Francisco)
(415) 329-4122

United States Mint (San Francisco)
(415) 744-9364

United States Postal Service (Anaheim/Fullerton/Santa Ana/City of Industry)
(818) 855-6339

United States Postal Service (Bakersfield)
(805) 392-6261

United States Postal Service (Marysville)
(916) 742-6429

United States Postal Service (Sacramento)
(916) 446-6944

United States Postal Service (Sacramento)
(916) 456-9675 (May contain same information as previous entry)

United States Postal Service (San Bernardino)
(909) 335-4339

United States Postal Service (San Diego)
(619) 221-3351

United States Postal Service (San Francisco)
(415) 550-5534   Ext. 1

Banks

Alliance Federal Credit Union (San Jose)
(408) 265-8380

Bank of California (San Francisco)
(415) 765-3535

Bank of San Diego (San Diego)
(619) 237-5457

Citibank/Citicorp (Oakland)
(510) 268-JOBS

Coast Federal Bank (Pasadena)
(818) 366-8730

Coast Federal Bank (San Francisco)
(415) 241-8730

Fidelity Federal Bank (Glendale)
(818) 917-2841

First Interstate Bank of California (Los Angeles)
(213) 614-4999

First Interstate Bank of California (San Diego)
(619) 699-3149

California

Grossmont Bank (San Diego)
  (619) 589-0536

Home Federal Bank F.S.B. (San Diego)
  (619) 450-8200

La Jolla Bank and Trust (La Jolla)
  (619) 458-2490

North County Bank (Escondido)
  (619) 737-6677

North Island Federal Credit Union (San Diego)
  (619) 656-6525   Ext. 169

Pacific Western Bank (San Jose)
  (408) 244-1700

Plaza Bank of Commerce (San Jose)
  (408) 294-8940

San Diego County Credit Union (San Diego)
  (619) 453-6941

San Diego National Bank (San Diego)
  (619) 233-1234   Ext. 337

San Diego Trust and Savings Bank (San Diego)
  (619) 557-2473

Santel Credit Union (San Diego)
  (619) 450-4400   Ext. 8

Union Bank (San Diego)
  (619) 230-3371

Union Bank (San Francisco)
  (415) 705-7013

West America Bank (San Rafael)
  (415) 382-6400

Western Federal Credit Union (Los Angeles)
(800) 669-9328 (Ext. 100, 7:30 A.M. to 5 P.M.,
Mon. through Fri., Pacific Time)

Education

Anaheim Unified School District (Anaheim)
(714) 635-4036 (Certified)

Cajon Valley School District (San Diego)
(619) 588-3222

California Institute of Technology (Pasadena)
(818) 796-2229

California Polytechnic State University (Pomona)
(909) 869-2100

California State University (Bakersfield)
(805) 664-2267

California State University (Fullerton)
(714) 773-3385

California State University (Hayward)
(510) 881-7474

California State University (Los Angeles)
(213) 343-3678

California State University (Sacramento)
(916) 278-6704

California State University (San Bernardino)
(909) 880-5139

California State University (San Marcos)
(619) 461-4101

California State University (Stanislaus)
(209) 667-3359

California

California Technical University (Pasadena)
  (818) 356-4661

California Technical University (San Luis Obispo)
  (805) 756-1533

Ceres Unified School District (Stanislaus)
  (209) 531-9936

Cerritos College (Norwalk)
  (310) 860-4714

Chaffey College (Rancho Cucamonga)
  (909) 941-2750

Citrus Community College (Glendora)
  (818) 914-8583

Claremont University Center (Claremont)
  (909) 621-9443

Coast Community College (Costa Mesa)
  (714) 432-5586 (Nonteaching)

Coast Community College (Costa Mesa)
  (714) 432-5526 (Teaching)

Compton Unified School District (Compton)
  (213) 537-1285

Cuesta College (San Luis Obispo)
  (805) 546-3127

Elk Grove Unified School District (Elk Grove)
  (916) 686-7782 (Certified)

Elk Grove Unified School District (Elk Grove)
  (916) 686-7781 (Classified)

Fontana Unified School District (San Bernardino)
  (909) 357-5627

Foothills/De Anza Community College (San Francisco)
(415) 949-6218

Garden Grove Unified School District (Garden Grove)
(714) 638-5627

Grant Joint Union High School District (Sacramento)
(916) 922-7968

Grossmont Cuyamaca College District (San Diego)
(619) 283-9478 (Tape F9)

La Mesa Spring School District (San Diego)
(619) 668-5700   Ext. 1

Lemon Grove School District (San Diego)
(619) 589-5603

Long Beach City College (Long Beach)
(310) 420-4050

Los Angeles City School District (Los Angeles)
(213) 742-7765 (Central/Nonteaching)

Los Angeles City School District (Los Angeles)
(213) 515-3143 (South/Nonteaching)

Los Angeles City School District (Los Angeles)
(213) 753-3321 (South-Central/Nonteaching)

Los Angeles City School District (Los Angeles)
(818) 997-2533 (Valley/Nonteaching)

Los Angeles City School District (Los Angeles)
(213) 478-2051 (West/Nonteaching)

Los Angeles City School District (Los Angeles)
(213) 625-6659 (Adult/Teaching)

Los Angeles City School District (Los Angeles)
(213) 625-6200 (Kindergarden through 12th Grade/Special Education/Teaching)

California

Los Angeles City School District (Los Angeles)
(213) 625-6846 (Preschool/Teaching)

Los Angeles Community College (Los Angeles)
(213) 891-2099 (Nonteaching)

Los Angeles Community College (Los Angeles)
(213) 891-2211 (Teaching)

Los Rios Community College District (Sacramento)
(916) 568-3011

Lucia Mar Unified School District (Arroyo Grande)
(805) 489-1724

Mira Costa College (San Diego)
(619) 757-2121   Ext. 8071

Modesto Unified School District (Modesto)
(209) 576-4103 (Certified)

Modesto Unified School District (Modesto)
(209) 576-4148 (Classified)

Montebello Unified School District (Montebello)
(213) 887-7921

Redlands Unified School District (Santa Maria)
(805) 793-1484

Sacramento Unified School District (Sacramento)
(916) 553-4224

Sacramento Unified School District (Sacramento)
(916) 553-4343 (May contain same information as previous entry)

Saddleback Community College District (Mission Viejo)
(714) 582-4469

San Bernardino Unified School District (San Bernardino)
(909) 888-9955

San Diego Community College (San Diego)
(619) 283-9478

San Diego State University (San Diego)
(619) 594-5861 (Administrative/Professional)

San Diego State University (San Diego)
(619) 594-5801 (Clerical/Secretarial)

San Diego State University (San Diego)
(619) 594-5850 (Technical/Research)

San Diego Unified School District (San Diego)
(619) 293-8002

San Francisco State University (San Francisco)
(415) 338-1177 (Alumni Network)

San Francisco State University (San Francisco)
(415) 338-1185 (Administrative/Management)

San Francisco State University (San Francisco)
(415) 338-1183 (Secretarial/Clerical)

San Francisco State University (San Francisco)
(415) 338-1184 (Technical/Maintenance)

San Francisco Unified School District (San Francisco)
(415) 241-6101 (Certified)

San Francisco Unified School District (San Francisco)
(415) 241-6162 (Classified)

San Francisco Unified School District (San Francisco)
(415) 241-6030 (Paraprofessional)

San Jose/Evergreen Community College District (San Jose)
(408) 223-6707

San Juan Unified School District (Sacramento)
(916) 971-7129 (Certified)

California

San Juan Unified School District (Sacramento)
(916) 971-7666 (Classified)

San Lorenzo Valley Unified School District (Santa Cruz)
(408) 335-9211

San Luis Coastal Unified School District (San Luis Obispo)
(805) 543-5075

San Mateo Community College (San Mateo)
(415) 574-6111

Santa Monica College (Santa Monica)
(310) 452-9336 (Academic)

Santa Monica College (Santa Monica)
(310) 452-9321 (Classified)

Sierra College (Rocklin)
(916) 781-0424

Solano Community College (Fairfield)
(707) 864-7129

Sonoma State University (Santa Rosa)
(707) 664-2168

Stanford University (Palo Alto)
(415) 725-5627

Sweetwater Union High School District (San Diego)
(619) 691-5574 (Nonteaching)

Sweetwater Union High School District (San Diego)
(619) 691-5408 (Teaching/Counseling)

University of California (Berkeley)
(510) 987-0824

University of California (Davis)
(916) 752-1760

University of California (Irvine)
(714) 856-5850

University of California (Los Angeles)
(310) 206-2957

University of California (Riverside)
(909) 787-3443

University of California (San Diego)
(619) 534-2374

University of California (San Francisco)
(415) 502-5627   Ext. 3

University of California (Santa Barbara)
(805) 893-3311

University of California (Santa Cruz)
(408) 459-2011

University of the Pacific (Stockton)
(209) 946-2621

University of Phoenix—Southern California Campus
(Santa Ana)
(714) 962-1460

University of Redlands (Santa Maria)
(805) 798-7482

University of San Diego (San Diego)
(619) 260-4626

University of San Francisco (San Francisco)
(415) 666-5600

University of Southern California (Los Angeles)
(213) 740-4728

Upland Unified School District (Pomona)
(909) 985-4984

California

Westmont College (Montecito)
(805) 565-6100

Hotels

Atlas Hotels Incorporated (San Diego)
(619) 299-2254

Bahia and Catamaran Resort Hotel (San Diego)
(619) 450-6204

Claremont Resort and Spa (Oakland)
(510) 549-8557

Doubletree Hotel (Burlingame)
(415) 348-4247

Embassy Suites Hotel (San Diego)
(619) 239-2400   Ext. 383

Fairmont Hotel (San Jose)
(408) 998-1900   Ext. 3113

Hilton Hotel (Long Beach)
(310) 983-3445

Hilton Hotel (San Diego)
(619) 543-9441

Hilton Hotel (San Francisco)
(415) 923-5068

Hilton Hotel (San Jose)
(408) 947-4455

Hotel Del Coronado (San Diego)
(619) 522-8158

Hotel Pan Pacific (San Diego)
(619) 338-3659

Holiday Inn (San Diego)
(619) 297-6026 (Hotel Circle)

Holiday Inn (San Diego)
(619) 232-3861 (ON THE HARBOR—Ask for Jobline)

Hyatt Regency Hotel (La Jolla)
(619) 552-6058

Hyatt Regency Hotel (Sacramento)
(916) 441-3111

Hyatt Regency Hotel (San Diego)
(619) 687-6000

Hyatt Islandia Hotel (San Diego)
(619) 221-4888

La Costa Resort and Spa (San Diego)
(619) 433-9675

Loew's Coronado Bay Resort (San Diego)
(619) 424-6190

Marriott Hotel (La Jolla)
(619) 552-8578

Marriott Hotel (San Diego)
(619) 230-8901

Marriott Hotel (Santa Clara)
(408) 980-0698

Parc Oakland Hotel (Oakland)
(510) 451-4000 (Ask for Jobline)

Radisson Hotel (San Jose)
(408) 441-8457

Red Lion Hotel (San Diego)
(619) 688-4004

Red Lion Hotel (San Jose)
(408) 437-2118

Sheraton Hotel (San Diego)
(619) 457-0974 (Grande Torrey Pines)

Sheraton Hotel (San Diego)
(619) 692-2793 (Harbor Island)

Westin Hotel (San Francisco)
(415) 872-8158

Westin Hotel (San Francisco)
(415) 774-0370 (St. Francis)

Medical/Hospitals

ASMCOPS Jobline (San Diego)
(619) 495-2052

Alta Bates-Herrick Hospital (Berkeley)
(510) 540-1305 (Nonnursing)

Alta Bates-Herrick Hospital (Berkeley)
(510) 540-1300 (Nursing)

Alvarado Hospital Medical Center (San Diego)
(619) 229-3303

Ames Healthcare (Los Angeles)
(800) 404-0400 (Within California)

Auburn Faith Community Hospital (Auburn)
(916) 885-1530

Bay Shore Medical Group (Torrance)
(310) 214-0811

Blue Cross/Blue Shield of California (Oxnard)
(805) 369-8499

California Dental Association (Sacramento)
(916) 443-4526

California Pacific Medical Center (San Francisco)
(415) 541-5898

Cardiometrics, Incorporated (San Francisco)
(415) 961-6993

Children's Hospital (San Diego)
(619) 576-5880 (General)

Children's Hospital (San Diego)
(619) 576-4019 (Nursing)

Children's Hospital of Orange County (Orange)
(714) 532-8500

Community Care Network (San Diego)
(619) 974-5033

Community Hospital (Chula Vista)
(619) 450-6245

Community Hospital of Central California (Fresno)
(209) 442-3981

Coronado Hospital (San Diego)
(619) 435-4519

Cottage Hospital (Santa Barbara)
(805) 569-7215

Davis Medical Center (San Francisco)
(415) 565-6104

Delta Memorial Hospital (Antioch)
(510) 779-7261

Downey Community Hospital (Downey)
(310) 904-5438

California

Eisenhower Medical Center (Palm Springs)
(619) 773-1358

FHP Health Care (Fountain Valley)
(800) 572-7522 (Within California)

FHP Health Care (San Diego)
(619) 688-5086

Foundation Health Corporation (Rancho Cordova)
(916) 631-5060

Fountain Valley Regional Hospital and Medical Center (Orange)
(714) 966-8108

Fremont Medical Center (Yuba City)
(916) 674-4074

Fremont Rideout Health Group (Sacramento)
(916) 751-4281

Green Hospital of Scripps Clinic (San Diego)
(619) 554-9740   Ext. 1

Grossmont Hospital (La Mesa)
(619) 450-6200

Harbor View Medical Center (San Diego)
(619) 235-3181

Hillside Hospital (San Diego)
(619) 450-6202

Hospice of Grossmont Hospital (La Mesa)
(619) 450-6200

Huntington Memorial Hospital (Pasadena)
(818) 397-5276

John Muir Medical Center (Walnut Creek)
(510) 947-5299 (Nonnursing)

John Muir Medical Center (Walnut Creek)
(510) 947-5266 (Nursing)

Kaiser Permanente (Anaheim)
(714) 572-8966

Kaiser Permanente (Antioch)
(510) 779-5265

Kaiser Permanente (Davis)
(916) 757-4170

Kaiser Permanente (Fremont)
(510) 795-3131

Kaiser Permanente (Fresno)
(209) 261-4840

Kaiser Permanente (Hayward)
(510) 784-4226

Kaiser Permanente (Livermore)
(510) 294-7177

Kaiser Permanente (Martinez)
(510) 372-1193

Kaiser Permanente (Oakland)
(510) 596-6140

Kaiser Permanente (Pasadena)
(818) 405-3280

Kaiser Permanente (Riverside)
(909) 353-4424

Kaiser Permanente (Roseville)
(916) 784-4463

Kaiser Permanente (Sacramento)
(916) 973-6846

California

Kaiser Permanente (San Diego)
(619) 528-3071

Kaiser Permanente (San Francisco)
(415) 202-2500

Kaiser Permanente (San Francisco)
(415) 929-4170 (May be same information contained in previous entry)

Kaiser Permanente (South Sacramento)
(916) 688-2369

Kaiser Permanente (Stockton)
(209) 476-3312

Kaiser Permanente (Vallejo)
(707) 648-6217

Kaiser Permanente (Walnut Creek)
(510) 295-4950

Kaiser Permanente (West Los Angeles)
(213) 857-2615

Las Encinas Hospital (Pasadena)
(818) 356-2648

Long Beach Memorial Medical Center (Long Beach)
(310) 595-2482 (Nonnursing)

Long Beach Memorial Medical Center (Long Beach)
(310) 595-3399 (Nursing)

Marin General Hospital (Marin)
(415) 925-7427

Med Clinic (Sacramento)
(916) 733-3465

Memorial Health Services (Long Beach)
(310) 933-2482 (Nonnursing)

Memorial Health Services (Long Beach)
(310) 933-3399 (Nursing)

Memorial Hospital Association (Modesto)
(209) 572-7290

Mercy American River Hospital (Carmichael)
(916) 484-2442

Mercy General Hospital (Bakersfield)
(805) 324-1500

Mercy General Hospital (Sacramento)
(916) 851-2227

Mercy General Hospital (San Diego)
(619) 260-7276

Mesa Vista Hospital (San Diego)
(619) 563-0184

Methodist Hospital (Sacramento)
(916) 423-4122

Mission Park Medical Center (San Diego)
(619) 967-4128

Mount Zion Medical Center (San Francisco)
(415) 502-5627

National Health Laboratories (San Diego)
(800) 859-6046 (Within California)

Nichols Institutes Laboratories (San Juan Capistrano)
(714) 728-4526

Pacificare Health Systems (Cypress)
(310) 917-4568

Palomar Medical Center (San Diego)
(619) 739-3960

California

Paradise Valley Hospital (National City)
(619) 470-4422

Parkview Community Hospital (Riverside)
(909) 352-5421

Pomerado Hospital (San Diego)
(619) 485-4191

Roseville Hospital (Roseville)
(916) 781-1090

St. Agnes Medical Center (Fresno)
(209) 449-5300

St. Francis Memorial Hospital (San Francisco)
(415) 353-6367

St. John's Hospital (Santa Monica)
(310) 829-8323

St. Joseph's Hospital (Orange)
(714) 744-8557

St. Joseph's Medical Center (Stockton)
(209) 467-6449

St. Jude Medical Center (Santa Ana)
(714) 992-3925

St. Luke's Hospital (San Francisco)
(415) 641-6591

St. Mary's Hospital and Medical Center (San Francisco)
(415) 750-5627

St. Mary's Medical Center (Long Beach)
(310) 491-9844

St. Rose Hospital (Hayward)
(510) 785-4291

St. Teresa Hospital (Santa Clara)
(408) 972-7290

San Antonio Community Hospital (Upland)
(909) 949-0719

San Diego Hospice (San Diego)
(619) 688-1500   Ext. 454

San Joaquin General Hospital (French Camp)
(209) 468-6034

Scripps Clinic and Research Foundation (San Diego)
(619) 554-8400

Scripps Memorial Hospital (Chula Vista)
(619) 691-7446

Scripps Memorial Hospital (Encinitas)
(619) 457-7430

Scripps Memorial Hospital (La Jolla)
(619) 457-7371

Scripps Memorial Hospital (San Diego)
(619) 554-8400

Sharp Health Care (San Diego)
(619) 450-6240   Ext. 3035 (Clerical)

Sharp Health Care (San Diego)
(619) 450-6240   Ext. 3034 (General)

Sharp Health Care (San Diego)
(619) 450-6240   Ext. 3032 (Management)

Sharp Health Care (San Diego)
(619) 450-6240   Ext. 3033 (Nursing)

Sharp Medical Center (Chula Vista)
(619) 450-6245

California

Sierra Nevada Memorial Hospital (Yuba City)
  (916) 274-6200

Stanford University Hospital (Palo Alto)
  (415) 723-5140

Summit Medical Center (Oakland)
  (510) 465-7688

Sutter Health (Sacramento)
  (916) 733-3733 (General)

Sutter Health (Sacramento)
  (916) 733-1733 (Nursing)

Torrance Memorial Medical Center (Torrance)
  (310) 517-4790

Tri-City Hospital (San Diego)
  (619) 450-6205

Tustin Hospital Medical Center (Tustin)
  (714) 669-5829

United Community Medical Services (Yuba City)
  (916) 674-4074

University of California Medical Center (Sacramento)
  (916) 752-1760

University of California Medical Center (San Diego)
  (619) 543-6250

University of Southern California Hospital (Los Angeles)
  (800) 955-6515

University of Southern California Hospital (Los Angeles)
  (213) 342-8801

Valley Children's Hospital (Fresno)
  (209) 224-3465

Villa View Community Hospital (San Diego)
(619) 582-3516 Ext. 299

Visiting Nurse Association (Orange)
(714) 549-2080

Visiting Nurse Association (Sacramento)
(916) 927-9278

Vista Hill Hospital (San Diego)
(619) 563-0184 Ext. 411

Washington Hospital (San Francisco)
(415) 791-3416

Miscellaneous

AC Transit (Oakland)
(510) 891-4782

Aerojet General Corporation (Sacramento)
(916) 355-4793

Allergan (Glendale)
(310) 576-4859

Allergan (Glendale)
(310) 917-4524 (May contain same information found in previous entry)

Allied-Signal Aerospace Company (Torrance)
(310) 512-3287

Allied-Signal Corporation (Livermore)
(510) 906-4147

Angeles Corporation (Los Angeles)
(310) 284-3504

Apple Computer (Cupertino)
(408) 996-1010 (Ask for Jobline, 8 A.M. to 5 P.M., Mon. through Fri., Pacific Time)

California

Apple Computer (Sacramento)
(916) 394-2675

ARCO (Los Angeles)
(213) 486-1285

Auspex Systems, Incorporated (San Jose)
(408) 492-0900

AVCO Financial Services (Orange)
(714) 553-1200

Aztech Laboratories (Oakland)
(510) 623-8988

Bechtel Corporation (San Francisco)
(415) 768-4449

Bergen Brunswig Corporation (Santa Ana)
(714) 385-4473

Brooktree Corporation (San Diego)
(619) 597-4322

Brush Wellman (Oakland)
(510) 795-1100

Burlington Air Express, Incorporated (Santa Ana)
(714) 752-1212

California Biotechnology (San Francisco)
(415) 962-5990

California Integrated Water Management (Sacramento)
(916) 255-2591

California Library Association (Northern California)
(916) 443-1222

California Library Association (Southern California)
(818) 797-4602

California Media and Library Educators Association
(San Francisco)
(415) 697-8832

California State Automobile Association (San Francisco)
(415) 565-2194

Capitol-EMI Music Incorporated (Los Angeles)
(213) 871-5763

Case Cave (Glendale)
(310) 917-2865

Central Contra Costa Sanitation District (Oakland)
(510) 372-6215

Chinese for Affirmative Action (San Francisco)
(415) 274-6766

Chisholm (San Jose)
(408) 559-1111

Cisco Systems (San Francisco)
(415) 903-7400

Citicorp Investment Company (Oakland)
(510) 268-JOBS

CLI (San Jose)
(408) 922-5454

Clorox Company (Oakland)
(510) 271-7615

Coca-Cola Bottling Company (Los Angeles)
(213) 746-5555   Ext. 4444

Community Interfaith Services (San Diego)
(619) 729-6391

Contel of California (Barstow)
(619) 245-0849

Continental Airlines (Los Angeles)
(310) 646-6955

California

Countrywide Servicing Exchange (Pasadena)
(818) 304-5925

Cox Cable Company (San Diego)
(619) 264-7051

Cubic Defense Systems, Incorporated (San Diego)
(619) 277-6780   Ext. 3300

DIP Services (San Francisco)
(415) 391-4540

Directors Mortgage (Riverside)
(909) 784-4830 (Ask for Jobline, 8:15 A.M. to
5:15 P.M., Mon. through Fri., Pacific Time)

Disneyland (Anaheim)
(714) 999-4407

Duncan Enterprises (Fresno)
(209) 291-4444   Ext. 596

East Bay Municipal Utility District (Oakland)
(510) 287-0742

Exicom Technologies (San Jose)
(408) 954-8977

Exploratorium (San Francisco)
(415) 561-0328

Failure Analysis Associates (San Francisco)
(415) 688-6700

Farmer's Insurance Group (Glendale)
(310) 917-5683

Ferretec (Oakland)
(510) 226-1216

FHP Incorporated (Fountain Valley)
(714) 378-5044

Fleetwood Enterprises Incorporated (Riverside)
(909) 788-5627

Fluor Daniel Corporation (Irvine)
(714) 975-5253

FMC Corporation, Defense Systems (Santa Clara)
(408) 289-4021

Foodmaker, Incorporated (San Diego)
(619) 571-2200

Fuji Optical Systems (San Jose)
(408) 866-5466

Gap Incorporated (San Francisco)
(415) 737-4495

GEICO (San Diego)
(619) 549-5687

General Atomics (San Diego)
(619) 455-2108

Golden Eagle Insurance (San Diego)
(619) 460-0310

Golden Gate Transit (San Francisco)
(415) 257-4545

Golden West (Santa Clara)
(408) 980-8669

Hank Fisher Properties (Sacramento)
(916) 922-2202

Hewlett-Packard Company (Sacramento)
(916) 786-6662

Hewlett-Packard Company (Sacramento)
(916) 785-4856 (TDD)

California

Hewlett-Packard Company (San Diego)
(619) 592-8444

H. M. Electronics (San Diego)
(619) 535-6035

H. M. T. (Oakland)
(510) 490-3100   Ext. 6950

Horizons Technology (San Diego)
(619) 292-8331   Ext. 860

Host International (San Diego)
(619) 542-1327

Household Credit (San Jose)
(408) 755-2929

IDENTEX (San Jose)
(408) 739-2000

Information Access Group (San Francisco)
(415) 378-5357

INTEL Corporation (Folsom)
(916) 356-0385

International Association of Business Communications
(San Francisco)
(415) 433-3400   Ext. 7

International Billing Services (Sacramento)
(916) 934-4577

International Business Machines (San Francisco)
(415) 545-3756

IVAC (San Diego)
(619) 458-7311

KFMB (San Diego)
(619) 495-8670

KGO Channel 7 (San Francisco)
(415) 954-7958

KITS (San Francisco)
(415) 626-9675

KOMAG Incorporated (Milpitas)
(408) 945-7014

KPIX Channel 5 (San Francisco)
(415) 765-8609

KQED Channel 9 (San Francisco)
(415) 553-2809

KRON Channel 4 (San Francisco)
(415) 561-8662   Ext. 1

L.A. Cellular (Long Beach)
(310) 403-8519

Levi Strauss and Company (San Francisco)
(415) 544-7828

Lockheed Corporation (Covina)
(818) 847-5980 (Hourly)

Lockheed Corporation (Covina)
(818) 847-4734 (Professional)

Long Beach Transit (Long Beach)
(310) 591-8234

Los Angeles Times (Los Angeles)
(213) 237-5406 (Clerical)

Los Angeles Times (Los Angeles)
(213) 237-5407 (Production, Skilled)

Los Angeles Times (Los Angeles)
(213) 237-5408 (Professional, Management, Technical)

California

Lucasarts (San Francisco)
(415) 662-1999

Mattel Incorporated (El Segundo)
(310) 524-3535

MCA Universal City Studios (Universal City)
(818) 777-5627

McDonnell Douglas Corporation (Long Beach)
(310) 593-9628 (General)

McDonnell Douglas Corporation (Long Beach)
(310) 593-9303 (Professional)

Media Alliance (San Francisco)
(415) 441-2620

Mervyn's (Hayward)
(510) 727-3322

MetWest Laboratories (San Jose)
(408) 288-9850

Minisystems (Burbank)
(310) 216-6101

Mitchell International (San Diego)
(619) 530-8915

Modesto Bee (Modesto)
(209) 578-2004

Modesto Irrigation District (Modesto)
(209) 526-7364

Molecular Biosystems, Incorporated (San Diego)
(619) 452-7393   Ext. 411

Monterey Bay Aquarium (Monterey)
(408) 648-4890

National Writer's Union (San Francisco)
  (415) 979-5522

Northrop Corporation (Pico Rivera)
  (310) 942-5001 (Advanced Systems Division—
  General)

Northrop Corporation (Hawthorne)
  (310) 332-2412 (Aircraft Division—General)

Northrop Corporation (Hawthorne)
  (310) 332-4986 (Aircraft Division—Technical)

Northrop Corporation (Los Angeles)
  (213) 600-4020 (General)

Orange County Register (Santa Ana)
  (714) 664-5099

Orchard Supply Hardware (San Jose)
  (408) Call-OSH

Pacific Bell (San Diego)
  (619) 268-6894

Pacific Bell (San Francisco)
  (415) 545-7823

Pacific Bell (San Francisco)
  (415) 542-0817 (Outside California)

Pacific Bell (San Francisco)
  (800) 924-JOBS (Within California)

Pacific Bell (San Jose)
  (408) 491-2347

Pacific Gas and Electric Company (San Francisco)
  (415) 973-5195 (College Recruitment)

Pacific Gas and Electric Company (San Francisco)
  (415) 973-3637 (General)

California

Pacific Gas and Electric Company (San Francisco)
(415) 973-7277 (General)

Pacific Gas and Electric Company (San Francisco)
(415) 545-7823 (Management)

Pacific Mutual Life Insurance (Newport Beach)
(714) 721-5050

Pactel Cellular (Irvine)
(714) 222-8888

Paramount Pictures Corporation (Los Angeles)
(213) 956-5216

PC World Communications (San Francisco)
(415) 978-3100

Preview Magazine (Santa Ana)
(714) 664-5099

Production International Services (El Dorado)
(916) 939-4577

Potpourri (San Jose)
(408) 748-1360

Redken Laboratories (Universal City)
(818) 922-2930

Resna Industries (Oakland)
(510) 651-1906

Roberta's Temporary Service (Oakland)
(510) 792-1279

Rohr Industries, Incorporated (San Diego)
(619) 691-2601

Roundtable Pizza (Fremont/Newark/Union City)
(510) 795-7212

Sacramento Bee (Sacramento)
(916) 423-4122

Sacramento Bee (Sacramento)
(916) 321-1625 (May contain same information as previous entry)

Sacramento Municipal Utility District (Sacramento)
(916) 732-6046

Sacramento Regional Transit (Sacramento)
(916) 321-3806

Safeway (Sacramento)
(916) 947-1153

Safeway (Statewide)
(800) 255-0812 (Within California)

San Diego Gas and Electric Company (San Diego)
(619) 654-1600

San Francisco Bay—San Andreas/Special Libraries Association (San Francisco)
(415) 856-2140

San Francisco Newspaper Agency (San Francisco)
(415) 777-7642   Ext. 1 (Selection No. 4)

Santa Cruz Seaside Company (Santa Cruz)
(408) 427-1777

Science Applications International (San Diego)
(619) 535-7536

SDSU Foundation (San Diego)
(619) 594-5703

Sea World of California (San Diego)
(619) 226-3861

SEI Tech Writing/CAD (San Jose)
(408) 433-1100

California

Sierra Club (San Francisco)
(415) 978-9085

SIGMA Circuits (Oakland)
(510) 727-9169

Southern California Chapter, Special Libraries
Association (Rosewood)
(818) 795-2145

Southern California Gas Company (Los Angeles)
(213) 244-1234

Southern Pacific (San Francisco)
(415) 541-1973

Sun Microsystem (Mountain View)
(800) 643-8300 (Ask for employment opportunities)

Systems Partners (Oakland)
(510) 254-3110

SYVA (San Jose)
(408) 239-2725

Technical Directions, Incorporated (San Diego)
(619) 297-5633

Teledyne Ryan Aeronautical (San Diego)
(619) 260-5425

Times Mirror Cable Television (Irvine)
(714) 660-8721

Times Mirror/Los Angeles Times (Los Angeles)
(213) 237-5700

Time-Warner, Incorporated (Burbank)
(310) 337-4914 (Other locations may be announced)

Tower Corporation (San Francisco)
(800) 339-5339 (Sunday 12 P.M. to 6 P.M.) (Within
California)

Tower Corporation (San Francisco)
(415) 788-8488 (Sunday 12 P.M. to 6 P.M.)

TRA (San Diego)
(619) 260-5425

TRW Military Electronic and Avionics Division (San Diego)
(619) 592-3908

UNISYS Corporation (Mission Viejo)
(714) 380-6606

United Airlines (San Francisco)
(415) 876-5422

USI Lighting (Oakland)
(510) 562-3500

VISA (San Francisco)
(415) 378-8299   Ext. 2

Walt Disney Company (Universal City)
(818) 560-6335 (Other locations may be announced)

Western Digital Corporation (Irvine)
(714) 932-5766

Wherehouse Entertainment (Torrance)
(310) 538-2314   Ext. 2541

Ziff Communications Company (San Francisco)
(415) 378-5357

Colorado

Cities

Arvada
 (303) 431-3008   Ext. 453

Aurora
 (303) 695-7222

Boulder
 (303) 441-3434

Brighton
 (303) 659-4050   Ext. 294 (8 A.M. to 5 P.M., Mon. through Fri., Mountain Time)

Broomfield
 (303) 469-0620

Commerce City
 (303) 289-3618

Denver (City and County)
 (303) 640-1234 (General)

Denver (City and County)
 (303) 640-3476 (General—May contain same information as previous entry)

Denver (City and County)
 (303) 640-3057 (TDD)

Denver (City and County)
 (303) 628-6339 (Water Department)

Englewood
 (303) 762-2304

Fort Collins
 (303) 493-2489   Ext. 161

Golden
 (303) 279-3331   Ext. 223

Grand Junction
 (303) 244-1449

Lakewood
 (303) 987-7777

Littleton
 (303) 795-3858

Longmont
 (303) 651-8710

Louisville
 (303) 666-6565   Ext. 413

Loveland
 (303) 962-2374

Northglenn
 (303) 450-8789

Thornton
 (303) 538-7240

Vail
 (303) 479-2343

Westminster
 (303) 650-0115

Wheat Ridge
 (303) 234-5927

Colorado

Counties

Adams (Brighton)
(303) 654-6075

Arapahoe (Aurora)
(303) 795-4480

Boulder (Boulder)
(303) 441-4555

Douglas (Castle Rock)
(303) 660-7420

Eagle (Eagle)
(303) 328-8891

El Paso (Colorado Springs)
(719) 520-7400

Jefferson (Golden)
(303) 271-8401

Larimer (Fort Collins)
(303) 498-7379

Mesa (Grand Junction)
(303) 244-1854   Ext. 1

Weld (Greeley)
(303) 352-1993

Weld Employment Services (Greeley)
(303) 353-3815   Ext. 6993 (Labor—8 A.M. to 5 P.M., Mon. through Fri.)

Weld Employment Services (Greeley)
(303) 353-3815   Ext. 6992 (Part-Time—8 A.M. to 5 P.M., Mon. through Fri.)

Weld Employment Services (Greeley)
(303) 353-3815   Ext. 6990 (Professional/Clerical—8 A.M. to 5 P.M., Mon. through Fri.)

Weld Employment Services (Greeley)
(303) 353-3815   Ext. 6991 (Service—8 A.M. to 5 P.M., Mon. through Fri.)

State

Colorado Mental Health Institute (Pueblo)
(719) 546-4612

Department of Labor (Statewide)
(303) 837-3986

Department of Revenue (Statewide)
(303) 866-3761

Department of Social Services (Statewide)
(303) 866-2255 (Office/Technical)

Department of Social Services (Statewide)
(303) 866-5985 (Professional/Administrative)

Department of Transportation (Statewide)
(303) 757-9623

Judicial Department (Statewide)
(303) 837-3671

State of Colorado (Statewide)
(303) 866-2431   Ext. 2 (Clerical)

State of Colorado (Statewide)
(303) 866-2431   Ext. 3 (Professional)

Wheat Ridge Regional Center (Wheat Ridge)
(303) 424-7791   Ext. 216

Wildlife (Statewide)
(303) 291-7527

Colorado

Federal

Air Force Academy (Colorado Springs)
(719) 472-2222

Central Intelligence Agency (Denver)
(800) 562-7242

Department of Commerce (Boulder)
(303) 497-6332

Environmental Protection Agency (Denver)
(303) 293-1564   Ext. 2 (Press #)

Federal Job Opportunities Center (Colorado Statewide)
(303) 969-7050

Federal Job Opportunities Center (Montana/Wyoming)
(303) 969-7052

Federal Job Opportunities Center (Utah)
(303) 969-7053

Federal Reserve Bank of Denver (Denver)
(303) 572-2308

Fort Carson (Colorado Springs)
(719) 579-3307

General Accounting Office (Denver)
(800) 967-5426   Ext. 2

General Services Administration (Denver)
(303) 236-7418

Geological Survey (Denver)
(303) 236-5846

Housing and Urban Development (Denver)
(303) 844-3967

Internal Revenue Service (Denver)
(303) 446-1087

National Park Service (Denver)
  (303) 969-2010

National Weather Service (Boulder)
  (303) 497-3950

Peterson Air Force Base (Colorado Springs)
  (719) 556-4111 (Appropriated)

United States Forest Service (Denver)
  (303) 275-5322

United States Postal Service (Colorado Springs)
  (719) 570-5316

United States Postal Service (Denver)
  (303) 297-6030

Western Area Power Administration (Denver)
  (303) 231-1148

Banks

Bank of Boulder (Boulder)
  (303) 938-4855

Bank One (Boulder)
  (303) 447-5849

Bank One (Denver)
  (303) 297-4200

Bellco Federal Credit Union (Denver)
  (303) 689-7884

Colorado National Bank (Denver)
  (303) 585-8600

Colorado National Bank (Denver)
  (303) 585-8610 (TDD)

First Interstate Bank (Denver)
  (303) 293-5777

Colorado

Norwest Banks (Denver)
(303) 863-5627

Security Service Federal Credit Union (Colorado Springs)
(719) 590-1022

Education

Adams County School District No. 12 (Thornton/Northglenn)
(303) 451-1561   Ext. 5

Adams County School District No. 14 (Commerce City)
(303) 286-8940

Auraria Higher Education Center (Denver)
(303) 556-8430

Aurora Public Schools (Aurora)
(303) 344-8060   Ext. 2

Boulder Valley School District (Boulder)
(303) 447-5199

Colorado College (Colorado Springs)
(719) 389-6888

Colorado State University (Fort Collins)
(303) 491-0618   Ext. 1001

Denver Public Schools (Denver)
(303) 764-3263

Douglas County School District (Castle Rock)
(303) 688-3195   Ext. 250 (7:30 A.M. to 5 P.M., Mon. through Fri., Mountain Time)

Poudre Valley School District (Fort Collins)
(303) 490-3628

University of Colorado (Boulder)
(303) 492-5442

University of Colorado (Colorado Springs)
(719) 593-3308

University of Denver (Denver)
(303) 871-3460

Hotels

Antlers Doubletree Hotel (Colorado Springs)
(719) 473-5600   Ext. 310

Broadmoor Hotel (Colorado Springs)
(719) 577-5858

Brown Palace Hotel (Denver)
(303) 298-1277

Denver Hilton South (Denver)
(303) 689-7042

Embassy Suites (Denver)
(303) 371-0249 (Airport)

Embassy Suites (Denver)
(303) 696-6644   Ext. 180 (Southeast)

Holiday Inn (Denver)
(303) 371-1862 (International Airport)

Holiday Inn (Northglenn)
(303) 452-4100   Ext. 155

Marriott City Center (Denver)
(303) 291-3644

Marriott Southeast (Denver)
(303) 758-7000 (Ask For Jobline)

Radisson Hotel (Denver)
(303) 893-0642

Colorado

Roadway Inn—Foothills (Denver)
(303) 238-6503 (When vacancies exist)

Sheraton Denver Tech Center (Denver)
(303) 779-1100   Ext. 170

Stapleton Plaza Hotel (Denver)
(303) 329-2762

Westin Hotel—Tabor Center (Denver)
(303) 572-9100 (Ask For Jobline)

Westin Resort (Vail)
(303) 479-7019

Medical/Hospitals

Aurora Presbyterian Hospital (Aurora)
(303) 360-3434

Aurora Regional Medical Center (Aurora)
(303) 695-2694 (Ancillary Opportunities)

Aurora Regional Medical Center (Aurora)
(303) 695-2695 (Nursing)

Avista Hospital (Louisville)
(303) 673-1262

Blue Cross/Blue Shield (Denver)
(303) 831-3105

Boulder Community Hospital (Boulder)
(303) 440-2323

Centennial Peaks Hospital (Louisville)
(303) 666-2094

Children's Hospital (Denver)
(303) 861-6449

Craig Rehabilitation Hospital (Englewood)
(303) 789-8497

Denver General Hospital (Denver)
(303) 640-1234

Denver General Hospital (Denver)
(303) 640-3057 (TDD)

Kaiser Permanente (Denver)
(303) 344-7666

Littleton Hospital (Littleton)
(303) 730-5859

Longmont United Hospital (Longmont)
(303) 651-5241

Lutheran Medical Center (Wheat Ridge)
(303) 425-2421

Memorial Hospital (Colorado Springs)
(719) 475-5113

National Jewish Hospital (Denver)
(303) 398-1740

North Suburban Medical Center (Thornton)
(303) 450-4550

Northern Colorado Medical Center (Greeley)
(303) 350-6565 (General)

Northern Colorado Medical Center (Greeley)
(303) 350-6397 (Nursing)

Penrose Community Hospital/Penrose Hospital/
St. Francis Hospital (Colorado Springs)
(719) 630-5237

Platte Valley Medical Center (Brighton)
(303) 654-8617

Porter Hospital (Denver)
(303) 778-5750 (Nonnursing)

Colorado

Porter Hospital (Denver)
(303) 778-5659 (Nursing)

Poudre Valley Hospital (Fort Collins)
(303) 495-7310

Presbyterian/St. Luke's Medical Center (Denver)
(303) 839-6163

Provident Health Partners (Denver)
(303) 629-3700

Provident Health Partners (Denver)
(303) 629-3701 (Rotary Telephone)

Rose Medical Center (Denver)
(303) 320-2196

St. Joseph's Hospital (Denver)
(303) 764-2265

St. Mary Corwin Hospital Regional Medical Center (Pueblo)
(719) 960-4888

Swedish Medical Center (Englewood)
(303) 788-6015

University Hospital (Denver)
(303) 270-3104

Miscellaneous

AAA Auto Club (Denver)
(303) 753-8800   Ext. 422

A Beautiful Clean (Denver)
(303) 331-2507

Airport Construction Jobs (Denver)
(800) 866-3382

American Telephone & Telegraph (Denver)
(800) 348-4313 (Management—8 A.M. to 8 P.M.,
Eastern Time)

American Telephone & Telegraph (Denver)
(800) 562-7288 (Trades and Office)

ATMEL (Colorado Springs)
(719) 540-1100

Auto-Trol (Northglenn)
(303) 252-2007

Bancroft Fire Protection District (Lakewood)
(303) 989-3968 (When vacancies exist)

Bullwhackers (Blackhawk/Central City/Golden)
(303) 271-2808

Burlington Northern Railroad (Denver)
(303) 220-3830

C&D Security (Colorado Springs)
(719) 597-1317

Career Track (Boulder)
(303) 447-2323   Ext. 1

Celestial Seasonings (Boulder)
(303) 581-1311

Citicorp/Diner's Club (Englewood)
(303) 649-2800   Ext. 3 (Then press 2)

Cobe Laboratories (Lakewood)
(303) 231-4440

Colorado Convention Center (Denver)
(303) 640-8119

Colorado Housing and Finance Authority (Denver)
(303) 297-7425

Colorado

Colorado Memory Systems (Loveland)
  (303) 635-6660

Colorado Plasti-Card (Denver)
  (303) 973-7688

Colorado Springs Public Library (Colorado Springs)
  (719) 531-6333   Ext. 8

Colorado State Library (Denver)
  (303) 866-6741

Confertech (Westminster)
  (303) 633-3002

Consolidated Collections Company (Denver)
  (303) 337-5847   Ext. 162 (Includes Electronic Job Filing System)

Consolidated Collections Company (Denver)
  (303) 337-5847   Ext. 181 (Includes Electronic Job Filing System)

Coors Brewing Company (Golden)
  (303) 277-2450

Coors Ceramics (Golden)
  (303) 277-4033

Cotter and Company (Denver)
  (303) 337-5847   Ext. 187 (Includes Electronic Job Filing System)

Current Incorporated (Colorado Springs)
  (719) 531-2520

Denver Museum of Natural History (Denver)
  (303) 370-6437

Denver Post (Denver)
  (303) 820-1820

DRCOG (Denver)
(303) 480-6714

Eastman Kodak (Windsor)
(303) 686-7611   Ext. 7939

EG&G Rocky Flats (Golden)
(303) 966-5606

Electro-Medics (Denver)
(303) 799-8420

Exabyte (Boulder)
(303) 447-7437

Fireplace Industries, Incorporated (Denver)
(303) 337-5847   Ext. 109 or 110 (Electronic Job Filing System available)

First Data (Denver)
(303) 337-5847   Ext. 150 or 185 (Electronic Job Filing System available)

Flatirons Structures (Longmont)
(303) 337-5847   Ext. 133 or 151 (Electronic Job Filing System available)

Frito-Lay (Denver)
(303) 371-7340

Funplex, Incorporated (Littleton)
(303) 337-5847   Ext. 139 (Electronic Job Filing System available)

Gates Rubber Company (Denver)
(303) 744-5900

Goodwill Industries (Denver)
(303) 650-7729   Ext. 29

Colorado

Guaranty National Insurance Company (Denver)
(303) 337-5847   Ext. 190 (Electronic Job Filing System available)

Hewlett-Packard (Colorado Springs)
(719) 590-2014

Hewlett-Packard (Englewood)
(303) 649-5877 (Sales office)

Hewlett-Packard (Fort Collins/Greeley/Loveland)
(800) 228-1399 (Press 3)

Hospital Shared Services (Denver)
(303) 871-7100

Hospitality Personnel (Denver)
(303) 292-8934

Human Resources of Colorado (Denver)
(303) 337-5847   Ext. 107 (Electronic Job Filing System available)

Information Handling Services (Denver)
(303) 397-2525

Interlink (Denver)
(303) 397-0922

International Business Machines (Boulder)
(303) 924-6502

J. D. Edwards Company (Denver)
(303) 488-4588

J. D. Edwards Company (Denver)
(800) 717-4588 (Outside Denver)

John Elway Dealerships (Denver)
(303) 337-5847   Ext. 103 (Electronic Job Filing System available)

Jones Intercable (Englewood)
(303) 784-8390

Keebler Company (Denver)
(303) 433-6221   Ext. 215

King Soopers (Denver)
(303) 778-3270

King Soopers (Denver)
(800) 283-1326 (Within Colorado)

KKTV (Colorado Springs)
(719) 630-1111   Ext. 5627

Lakewood Country Club (Lakewood)
(303) 337-5847   Ext. 163 (Electronic Job Filing System available)

Martin Marietta Astronautics Division (Denver)
(303) 977-2720

MCI—Systems Engineering (Colorado Springs)
(800) 766-2848

MCI West (Englewood)
(303) 773-4302

MCI West (Englewood)
(800) 288-9378

MDC Holdings (Denver)
(303) 337-5847   Ext. 167 (Electronic Job Filing System available)

Medical Group Management Association (Englewood)
(303) 337-5847   Ext. 155 (Electronic Job Filing System available)

Metropolitan Club (Denver)
(303) 337-5847   Ext. 135 (Electronic Job Filing System available)

Colorado

Metrum Information Storage (Littleton)
(303) 773-4695

Micro-Motion (Boulder)
(303) 530-8000

Mile High Honda/Acura (Denver)
(303) 337-5847   Ext. 182 (Electronic Job Filing System available)

Mountain Plains Library Association (Statewide)
(605) 677-5757

Mountain Plains Library Association (Statewide)
(800) 356-7820 (Within Colorado)

National Renewable Energy Laboratory (Golden)
(303) 628-4650

Navajo Shippers, Incorporated (Denver)
(303) 337-5847   Ext. 182 (Electronic Job Filing System available)

NCAR/UCAR (Boulder)
(303) 497-8707

Neodata (Boulder)
(303) 665-1645

Nobel/Sysco (Denver)
(303) 337-5847   Ext. 156 (Electronic Job Filing System available)

Northern Telecom (Englewood)
(303) 850-2662

Oppenheimer Management (Denver)
(303) 671-3558

Pepsi Cola (Denver)
(303) 299-4599

Pizza Hut (Colorado Springs)
(719) 531-6637

The Product Line (Englewood)
(303) 743-9530 (Customer Service)

The Product Line (Englewood)
(303) 743-9531 (Telemarketing)

Professional Search and Placement (Denver)
(303) 741-0748

Prologue (Westminster)
(303) 654-6454

Public Service Company of Colorado (Denver)
(303) 571-7563

Regional Transportation District (Denver)
(303) 299-2309

Risk Removal, Incorporated (Denver)
(303) 296-9471 (Ask for Job Line)

Risk Removal, Incorporated (Fort Collins)
(303) 495-6306 (Ask for Job Line)

Safeco Insurance Company (Denver)
(303) 239-0193

Safeway (Denver)
(303) 843-7828

Samsonite (Denver)
(303) 373-7473

Security Life (Denver)
(303) 860-2110

Shepard's McGraw-Hill (Colorado Springs)
(719) 481-7432

Colorado

Society for Technical Communications (Denver)
(303) 238-5352

Stanley Aviation (Denver)
(303) 340-5200   Ext. 504

Starbucks Coffee (Denver)
(303) 721-8191

Storage Technology (Louisville)
(303) 673-5300

Synergen Incorporated (Boulder)
(303) 441-5544

TRW-SIG (Colorado Springs)
(719) 570-8009

Tele-Communication Incorporated (TCI) (Englewood)
(303) 267-6650

Teledial America (Denver)
(303) 337-5847   Ext. 148 (Electronic Job Filing System available)

Telelink (Denver)
(303) 295-7052

Time-Life Libraries (Denver)
(303) 337-5847   Ext. 141 (Electronic Job Filing System available)

Time-Warner Cable (Englewood)
(303) 799-1200   Ext. 4216

UNIPAC (Denver)
(303) 696-5616

United Airlines (Denver)
(303) 398-4551 (Ground Support)

U.S. Olympic Center (Colorado Springs)
(719) 578-4680

U.S. West (Denver)
(303) 896-7683

Valleylab (Boulder)
(303) 530-6346

Valleylab (Boulder)
(800) 638-8367

Volunteers of America (Denver)
(303) 297-0408   Ext. 80

Wagner Equipment Company (Denver)
(303) 739-3010   Ext. 2

Walter Drake (Colorado Springs)
(719) 637-4992

Yellow Cab (Denver)
(303) 337-5847   Ext. 106 (Electronic Job Filing System available)

Connecticut

Cities

Manchester
  (203) 647-3076

New Haven
  (203) 787-8265

Education

Connecticut College (New London)
  (203) 439-2069

University of Connecticut (Storrs)
  (203) 486-2466

Medical/Hospitals

Manchester Memorial Hospital (Manchester)
  (203) 647-6424

Rockville General Hospital (Vernon)
  (203) 872-5200

Miscellaneous

Aerotek (New Haven)
  (203) 925-4247

Aerotek (New Haven)
  (203) 925-4242 (May contain same information as previous entry)

American Telephone & Telegraph (Statewide)
(800) 858-5417

Connecticut Library Association (Statewide)
(203) 645-8090

New England Library Association (Statewide)
(617) 738-3148

New York Chapter, Special Library Association
(Statewide)
(212) 740-2007

Southern New England Telephone Company
(Statewide)
(800) 922-1252 (New England States Only)

Delaware

Cities

Wilmington
 (302) 571-4666

Counties

Kent (Dover)
 (302) 739-4434

State

Delaware Department of Labor (Wilmington)
 (302) 577-2750

Delaware Job Service Hotline (Dover)
 (302) 739-4434

Banks

American Express Centurion Bank (Newark)
 (302) 454-2562

Delaware Trust Company (Milford)
 (302) 421-7104

Education

University of Delaware (Wilmington)
 (302) 831-2100 (Professional)

University of Delaware (Wilmington)
 (302) 831-6612 (Salaried)

Medical/Hospitals

Medical Center of Delaware (Wilmington)
(302) 428-6284

Milford Memorial Hospital (Milford)
(302) 424-5519

Miscellaneous

Bell Atlantic Network Services (Statewide)
(800) 462-1691

Delaware Library Association (Statewide)
(302) 739-4748   Ext. 69

Delaware Library Association (Statewide)
(800) 282-8696 (Within Delaware)

Delmarva Power and Light Company (Wilmington)
(302) 429-3450

Drexel University—College of Information (Statewide)
(215) 895-1672

Dupont Company (Wilmington)
(302) 992-6349

Hercules, Incorporated (Wilmington)
(302) 594-6122

Maryland Library Association (Statewide)
(410) 685-5760

New Jersey Library Association (Statewide)
(609) 695-2121

Pennsylvania Cooperative Jobline (Statewide)
(717) 234-4646

W. L. Gore and Associates (Wilmington)
(302) 738-3671

District of Columbia

City

Washington Convention Center
 (202) 371-4498

Washington, DC—Alcohol and Drug Abuse Services
 Administration
 (202) 783-1300

Washington, DC—Metropolitan Washington Council
 of Governments Library Council
 (202) 962-3712

Federal

Action
 (202) 606-5000

Bureau of National Affairs
 (202) 452-4335

Commodity Futures Trading Commission
 (202) 254-3346

Department of Energy
 (202) 586-4333

Department of Health and Human Services
 (202) 619-2560

Department of Housing and Urban Development
 (202) 708-3203

Department of Justice
(202) 514-6818

Department of Navy
(202) 433-4930 (Domestic)

Department of State
(202) 647-7284

Department of Transportation
(202) 366-9397

Environmental Protection Agency
(202) 260-5055

Executive Office of the President
(202) 395-5892
(202) 260-3141 (TDD)

Federal Aviation Administration
(202) 267-3226

Federal Aviation Administration
(202) 267-8007   Ext. 3 (May contain information found in previous entry)

Federal Aviation Administration
(202) 267-3229   Ext. 3 (May contain information found in previous entries)

Federal Deposit Insurance Corporation
(202) 898-8890

Federal Emergency Management Agency
(202) 646-3244   Ext. 1 (Then press 1)

Federal Energy Regulatory Commission
(202) 219-2791

Federal National Mortgage Association
(202) 752-5627

District of Columbia

Federal National Mortgage Association
(202) 752-3644 (TDD)

Federal Reserve Board
(202) 452-3038

Federal Trade Commission
(202) 326-2020

General Accounting Office
(202) 275-6092

Immigration and Naturalization Service
(202) 514-4301

Internal Revenue Service Chief Counsel
(202) 622-1029

International Monetary Fund
(202) 623-7422

Library of Congress
(202) 707-5295

Merit Systems Protection Board
(202) 254-8013

National Endowment for the Arts
(202) 682-5405

National Endowment for the Arts
(202) 682-5799 (May contain information found in previous entry)

National Gallery of Art
(202) 842-6298

National Park Service
(202) 619-7111

National Science Foundation
(202) 357-7735

Office of Management and Budget
(202) 395-5892

Office of Personnel Management
(202) 606-2700

Peace Corps
(202) 606-3214

Small Business Administration
(800) 827-5722

Smithsonian Institute
(202) 287-3102

United States Bureau of Alcohol, Tobacco and Firearms
(202) 927-8423

United States Bureau of Indian Affairs
(202) 208-2682

United States Information Agency
(202) 619-4539

United States Treasury Department
(202) 622-1029

Veterans Affairs Medical Center
(202) 745-8000

Voice of America
(202) 619-0909

Washington Navy Yard
(202) 433-4930

Banks

Citicorp/Citibank
(202) 429-7760

World Bank Group
(202) 473-8151

Education

American University
 (202) 885-2639

Brookings Institute
 (202) 797-6219

Catholic University
 (202) 319-5263

Gallaudet University
 (202) 651-5358

Gallaudet University
 (202) 651-5359 (TDD)

Howard University and Hospital
 (202) 806-7711

National Education Association
 (202) 822-7642

Hotels

Choice International Hotels/Manner Care Incorporated
 (800) 348-2041

Washington Hilton and Towers
 (202) 797-5818

Medical/Hospitals

Children's National Medical Center
 (202) 745-2600

Columbia Hospital for Women Medical Center
 (202) 293-5149

Georgetown University Hospital
 (202) 784-2683

Greater Southeast Hospital
(202) 574-6983

Group Health Association
(202) 364-2080

Hadley Memorial Hospital
(202) 574-5726

Howard University and Hospital
(202) 806-7712

Kaiser Permanente Medical Center
(800) 326-4005

National Rehabilitation Hospital
(202) 877-1700

Providence Hospital
(202) 269-7923

Sibley Memorial Hospital
(202) 364-8665

Washington Hospital Center
(202) 877-7451

Miscellaneous

American Film Institute
(202) 639-2150

American Telephone & Telegraph
(800) 562-7288 (Utility)

American Telephone & Telegraph
(800) 562-7665 (TDD)

Bell Atlantic Network Services
(800) 967-5422

District of Columbia

Bell Atlantic Network Services
(202) 508-2836

Black Entertainment Television
(202) 636-2400   Ext. 3

B'nai B'rith National Headquarters
(202) 857-6510

Cable News Network
(202) 898-7900

Cable Satellite Public Affairs Network
(202) 626-7983

Cafritz Company
(202) 862-6820

Chesapeake and Potomac Telephone
(202) 508-2836

Chesapeake and Potomac Telephone
(202) 347-7070 (May contain information found in previous entry)

Duron Paints and Wall Coverings
(800) 72-Duron   Ext. JOBS

Friends of the National Zoo
(202) 673-4640

GTS Computer Services
(800) 338-4487

MCI
(800) 777-6063

National Broadcasting Co./WRC-TV Channel 4
(202) 885-4058

National Public Radio
(202) 822-2777

National Research, Incorporated
(202) 686-9740

National Research, Incorporated
(202) 686-9743 (May contain information found in previous entry)

Potomac Electric and Power Co.
(202) 872-2100

Riggs National Corporation
(202) 835-6423   Ext. 2

Southland Corp. (7-11 and High's)
(800) 562-0711

U.S. News and World Report
(202) 955-2104

Urban Institute
(202) 857-8604

Washington Personnel Association
(202) 966-5627

Washington Post
(202) 334-5350

Washington Times
(202) 636-4700

WHUR Television and Radio
(202) 806-3696   Ext. 1

WJLA-TV Channel 7
(202) 364-7914

WTTG-Fox TV Channel 5
(202) 895-3233

WUSA-TV Channel 9
(202) 895-5895

Florida

Cities

Altamonte Springs
 (407) 830-0363

Boca Raton
 (407) 393-7981

Boca Raton
 (407) 367-7043 (TDD)

Daytona Beach
 (904) 258-3167

Delray Beach
 (407) 243-7085

Fort Lauderdale
 (305) 761-5317

Fort Myers
 (813) 334-1251

Gainesville
 (904) 334-2099

Hialeah
 (305) 883-8057

Hollywood
 (305) 921-3292

Jacksonville
 (904) 630-1144 (General)

Jacksonville
  (904) 630-3095 (Port Authority)

Miami
  (305) 579-2400

National Beach
  (305) 868-2929

North Miami
  (305) 895-8095

Oakland Park
  (305) 561-6255

Orlando
  (407) 246-2178 (General)

Orlando
  (407) 246-2473 (Police Department)

Plantation
  (305) 797-2298

St. Petersburg
  (813) 893-7033

Tallahassee
  (904) 891-8219

Tamarac
  (305) 726-8980

Tampa
  (813) 223-8115

Counties

Broward (Fort Lauderdale)
  (305) 357-6450

Dade (Miami)
  (305) 375-1871

Florida

Osceola (Kissimmee)
 (407) 847-1444

Orange (Orlando)
 (407) 836-5674 (General)

Orange (Orlando)
 (407) 836-4071 (Sheriff's Office)

Palm Beach (West Palm Beach)
 (407) 355-3947

Pinellas (Clearwater)
 (813) 462-3745

Sarasota (Sarasota)
 (813) 951-5495

State

Department of Health (Miami)
 (305) 377-5747

Department of Natural Resources (Tallahassee)
 (904) 487-0436

Federal

Federal Job Information Center (Orlando)
 (407) 648-6148

Federal Reserve Bank of Atlanta (Miami)
 (305) 471-6480

Patrick Air Force Base (Orlando)
 (407) 494-7661

Tyndall Air Force Base (Panama City)
 (904) 283-2006

Pensacola Naval Air Station (Pensacola)
 (904) 452-3111

United States Government Courts (Miami)
(305) 530-7834

Banks

American National Bank of Florida (Jacksonville)
(904) 396-8494

BancBoston Mortgage Corporation (Jacksonville)
(904) 281-3814

Barnett Bank, Inc. (Jacksonville)
(904) 791-7500

Barnett Bank, Inc. (Tampa)
(813) 225-8761

Barnett Bank of Dade County (Miami)
(305) 374-4473

Barnett Bank of South Florida (Miami)
(305) 558-4473

Capitol Bank (Miami)
(305) 270-3930

Chase Bank (Tampa)
(813) 881-2225

City National Bank (Hillsborough)
(813) 224-2002 (Nonofficer)

City National Bank (Hillsborough)
(813) 224-2001 (Officer)

City National Bank (Miami)
(305) 868-2929

City National Bank (Pinellas)
(813) 833-3011

Fortune Bank (Clearwater)
(813) 328-3050

Glendale Federal Bank (Orlando)
(800) 669-1562

Intercontinental Bank (Miami)
(305) 377-6901

NA Banco (Fort Lauderdale)
(305) 846-1546

Nationsbank (Miami)
(305) 577-JOBS

Nationsbank (Miami)
(800) 525-8154

Nationsbank (Palm Beach)
(305) 765-2887

Nationsbank (Orlando)
(407) 648-2820

Nationsbank (Tampa)
(813) 224-5921

Sunbank (Miami)
(305) 579-7001

Sunbank, South Florida (Fort Lauderdale)
(305) 765-7100

Education

Florida A&M University (Tallahassee)
(904) 561-2436

Florida Community College of Jacksonville
(Jacksonville)
(904) 632-3161

Florida International University (Miami)
(305) 348-2500

Miami-Dade Community College (Miami)
(305) 237-2050

University of Central Florida (Orlando)
(407) 823-2778

University of Florida (Gainesville)
(904) 392-4631

University of Miami (Coral Gables)
(305) 284-6918

University of Miami School of Medicine (Miami)
(305) 547-6999

Valencia Community College (Orlando)
(407) 299-4943

Hotels

Boca Raton Bridge Hotel (Boca Raton)
(407) 368-9500

Bonaventure Resort and Spa (Fort Lauderdale)
(305) 389-0185

Doral Resort and Country Club (Miami)
(305) 591-6424

Grand Bay Hotel (Coconut Grove)
(305) 858-9600   Ext. 7918

Hyatt Regency (Miami)
(305) 373-5627

Hyatt Regency (Orlando)
(407) 239-3899

Hyatt Regency (Orlando)
(407) 396-5001

Florida

Palm-Aire Spa Resort (North Pompano Beach)
(305) 968-2720

The Peabody (Orlando)
(407) 352-2681

Pier 66 (Fort Lauderdale)
(305) 728-3583

Westin Hotels/Walt Disney World Swan (Orlando)
(407) 934-1660

Medical/Hospitals

All Children's Hospital (St. Petersburg)
(813) 892-4480

AMI Memorial Hospital (Tampa)
(813) 876-7153

Baptist Hospital (Miami)
(305) 598-5999

Baptist Medical Center (Jacksonville)
(904) 393-2255

Bascom Palmer Eye Institute/Anne Bates Leach Eye Hospital/University of Miami (Coral Gables)
(305) 326-6JOB

Bayfront Medical Center (St. Petersburg)
(813) 893-6080

Blue Cross/Blue Shield of Florida (Jacksonville)
(904) 791-6538

Bon Secours St. Joseph Hospital (Port Charlotte)
(813) 764-2006

CIGNA Health Plan (Tampa)
(813) 828-6525

Delray Community Hospital (Delray Beach)
(407) 495-3459

East Pasco Medical Center (Dade City)
(800) 326-6191 (Press 3)

Good Samaritan Medical Center (West Palm Beach)
(407) 650-6101

HCA Northwest Regional Hospital (Margate)
(305) 975-6411

Hialeah Hospital (Miami)
(305) 835-4106

Holy Cross Hospital (Fort Lauderdale)
(305) 776-3001

Hospice (Tampa)
(813) 877-2200

Humana Hospital (Brandon)
(813) 681-0514

Humana Hospital (Jacksonville)
(904) 521-1199

Humana Hospital (Tampa)
(813) 521-5013

Kissimmee Memorial Hospital (Kissimmee)
(407) 933-6671

Life Concepts (Tampa)
(813) 654-7780

Memorial Hospital (Tampa)
(813) 876-7153

Memorial Medical Center (Jacksonville)
(904) 399-6702

Florida

Mental Health Care, Inc. (Tampa)
 (813) 237-4080   Ext. 305

Mercy Del Rey Home Care (Miami)
 (305) 674-2919

Mercy Hospital (Miami)
 (305) 285-2900

Methodist Medical Center (Jacksonville)
 (904) 798-8651

Miami Children's Hospital (Miami)
 (305) 662-8295

Morton Plant Hospital (Clearwater)
 (813) 462-7342

Mount Sinai Medical Center (Miami Beach)
 (305) 674-2503

Orlando Regional Health Care System (Orlando)
 (407) 841-5186

Orlando Regional Health Care System (Orlando)
 (800) 327-8402 (Press 1)

Palms of Pasadena Hospital (St. Petersburg)
 (813) 341-7007

Pan American Hospital (Miami)
 (305) 267-8544

Parkway Regional Medical Center (North Miami Beach)
 (305) 654-5223

Pembroke Pines Hospital (Fort Lauderdale)
 (305) 963-8498

Pembroke Pines Hospital (Fort Lauderdale)
 (305) 967-2043 (TDD)

Rehabilitation Institute of Sarasota (Sarasota)
(813) 924-0621

Riverside Clinic (Jacksonville)
(904) 387-7607

Riverside Hospital (Jacksonville)
(904) 381-7800

St. Anthony's Hospital (St. Petersburg)
(813) 894-0221

St. Joseph's Hospital (Tampa)
(813) 870-4539

Sarasota Memorial Hospital (Sarasota)
(813) 952-2540

Shands Hospital at the University of Florida
(Gainesville)
(800) 325-0367 (Press 1)

Shriner's Hospital for Crippled Children
(St. Petersburg)
(813) 977-4613

South Florida Baptist Hospital (Plant City)
(813) 281-7645

South Seminole Community Hospital (Orlando)
(407) 767-1200   Ext. 257

Tampa General Hospital (Tampa)
(813) 253-4100

Town and Country Hospital (Tampa)
(813) 885-6666   Ext. 196

University Community Hospital (St. Petersburg)
(813) 972-7830

University General Hospital (Tampa)
(813) 399-3228

Florida

Vencor Hospital (Tampa)
(813) 839-6341   Ext. 244

Visiting Nurses (St. Petersburg)
(800) 289-1696

Watson Clinic (Lakeland)
(813) 680-7900

Miscellaneous

Aero Corporation (Jacksonville)
(904) 755-1900

American Express/Travel Services (Jacksonville)
(904) 565-5050

Bankers Insurance Group (St. Petersburg)
(813) 577-2553

Carnival Cruise Lines, Inc. (Miami)
(305) 471-4780

Carnival Cruise Lines, Inc. (Miami)
(800) 553-0214 (TDD)

Coiffeur Transocean Inc. (Miami)
(305) 358-8739

Colorado Prime (Clearwater)
(813) 791-1101

Colorado Prime (Tampa)
(813) 855-5751

Commodore Cruise Line (Miami)
(305) 529-3222

Cordis Corporation (Miami)
(305) 824-2160

Coulter Electronics (Hialeah)
(305) 883-6825

Florida Power Corporation (St. Petersburg)
(813) 866-5627

Florida Power and Light Company (Miami)
(305) 347-7074

Florida State Library (Tallahassee)
(904) 488-5232

Florida Times-Union (Jacksonville)
(904) 359-4588

Freedom Square (Tampa)
(813) 397-9128

Greater Orlando Aviation Authority (Orlando)
(407) 825-2253

GTE Florida Incorporated (Tampa)
(813) 224-4211

Home Shopping Network (Tampa)
(813) 573-0500

Humana Health Care Plans (Jacksonville)
(904) 296-7070

Humana Health Care Plans (Tampa)
(813) 281-6077

Independent Life and Accident Insurance Company
(Jacksonville)
(904) 358-5392

J. Eckerd Corporation (Largo)
(813) 398-8443

J. I. Kislak Mortgage (Miami)
(305) 364-4117

Jim Walter Corporation (Tampa)
(813) 873-4235

Florida

Loan America Financial Corporation (Miami)
(305) 383-4784

Majestic Towers (St. Petersburg)
(813) 381-5411   Ext. 4153

Manpower Temporary Service (Orlando)
(407) 628-WORK

Morrison's Cafeteria (St. Petersburg)
(813) 441-6422

M.R.S. Power Systems (Jacksonville)
(904) 799-4800

NCCCI (Boca Raton)
(407) 997-4110

Nutmeg Mills (St. Petersburg)
(813) 893-8409

Orlando Utilities Commission (Orlando)
(407) 423-9191

Palm Beach Post (Palm Beach)
(305) 820-4567   Ext. 1090

Progressive Auto Insurance (Tampa)
(813) 623-1781   Ext. 2505

Ryder Systems, Inc. (Miami)
(305) 593-3066

St. Petersburg Times (St. Petersburg)
(813) 893-8404

Sea World of Florida (Orlando)
(407) 363-2612

Southern Bell (Fort Lauderdale)
(305) 776-3633

Southern Bell (Miami)
(305) 363-3020

Southern Bell (St. Augustine)
(904) 350-3026

Tampa Tribune (Tampa)
(813) 259-7650

Tech Data (Tampa)
(813) 539-7429

Telecredit (Tampa)
(813) 886-5000   Ext. 1

United Telephone Company of Florida (Altamonte Springs)
(407) 263-5405

Universal Studios Florida (Orlando)
(407) 363-8080

USAA (Tampa)
(813) 286-5883

U.S. Home Corporation (Clearwater)
(813) 796-0447

U.S. Home Corporation (Clearwater)
(800) 282-3449 (Outside Area Code/Within Florida)

U.S. Home Corporation (Clearwater)
(800) 237-2604 (Outside Florida)

Walt Disney World (Lake Buena Vista)
(407) 828-3088

Westinghouse Electric Corporation (Orlando)
(407) 281-2500

Georgia

Cities

Athens
 (706) 613-3100

Atlanta
 (404) 330-6456

Columbus
 (706) 571-4738

Macon
 (912) 751-2733

Marietta
 (404) 528-0593

Savannah
 (912) 651-6488

Counties

Chatham (Savannah)
 (912) 652-7931

Clarke (Athens)
 (404) 613-3100

Clayton (Jonesboro)
 (404) 473-5800

Cobb (Marietta)
 (404) 528-2555

De Kalb (Atlanta)
 (404) 371-2331

Douglas (Douglasville)
(404) 920-7363

Gwinnett (Lawrenceville)
(404) 822-7930

Rockdale (Conyers)
(404) 929-4157

State

Georgia Department of Corrections (Statewide)
(404) 656-4593

Georgia Ports Authority (Savannah)
(912) 964-3970

State of Georgia (Atlanta)
(404) 656-2724

Federal

Army Corps of Engineers (Savannah)
(912) 652-5763

Centers for Disease Control (Atlanta)
(404) 332-4577   Ext. 6

Environmental Protection Agency (Atlanta)
(800) 833-8130 (Georgia Only)

Federal Job Information Center (Atlanta)
(404) 331-4315

Federal Law Enforcement Training Center (Glynco)
(912) 267-2287

Federal Reserve Bank (Atlanta)
(404) 521-8767

Fort Benning (Columbus)
(706) 545-7084

Georgia

Fort Gordon (Augusta)
(706) 791-7766

Fort Stewart (Savannah)
(912) 762-5627

General Services Administration (Atlanta)
(404) 331-5102

Kings Bay Naval Station (Savannah)
(800) 544-1707

Moody Air Force Base (Valdosta)
(912) 333-3133

Office of Personnel Management College Job Hotline
(Statewide)
(900) 990-9200

Resolution Trust Corporation (Atlanta)
(404) 225-5708

United States Internal Revenue Service (Atlanta)
(404) 455-2455

United States Internal Revenue Service (Atlanta)
(404) 331-2486 (May contain information found in previous entry)

United States Postal Service (Savannah)
(912) 235-4629

Veterans Administration Medical Center (Augusta)
(706) 823-2204

Banks

Bank South (Atlanta)
(404) 529-4285

Columbia Bank and Trust (Columbus)
(706) 649-4758

C&S Nationsbank (Atlanta)
(404) 491-4530

C&S Nationsbank (Savannah)
(912) 944-3307

First American Bank FSB (Atlanta)
(404) 951-4010

First Union National Bank of Georgia (Decatur)
(404) 371-4177

Georgia Federal Bank FSB (Atlanta)
(404) 330-7188

Homebanc Federal Savings Bank (Atlanta)
(404) 303-4114

Prime Bank (Atlanta)
(404) 370-8566

South Trust (Atlanta)
(404) 951-4010

Trust Company Bank (Atlanta)
(404) 588-7118

Wachovia Bank (Atlanta)
(404) 841-7077

Education

Agnes Scott College (Atlanta)
(404) 371-6383

Emory University (Atlanta)
(404) 727-7611

Georgia Institute of Technology (Atlanta)
(404) 894-4592

Georgia State University (Atlanta)
(404) 651-4270

Georgia

Mercy University (Macon)
  (912) 752-2785

Spelman College (Atlanta)
  (404) 223-5627

University of Georgia (Athens)
  (706) 542-5720 (Clerical)

University of Georgia (Athens)
  (706) 542-8722 (Lab and Research)

University of Georgia (Athens)
  (706) 542-5769 (Service and Maintenance)

University of Georgia (Athens)
  (706) 542-5781 (Technical and Professional)

Hotels

Holiday Inns (Statewide)
  (404) 608-5627   Ext. 3

Hyatt Regency (Atlanta)
  (404) 588-3746

Sheraton Colony Square (Atlanta)
  (404) 873-5685

Medical/Hospitals

American Red Cross (Atlanta)
  (404) 892-1078

Atlanta Medical Association (Atlanta)
  (404) 872-3708 (Ask for Job Line)

Augusta Regional Medical Center (Augusta)
  (706) 868-2418

Blue Cross/Blue Shield of Georgia (Atlanta)
  (404) 529-4285

Blue Cross/Blue Shield of Georgia (Columbus)
(706) 571-5100

Brawner Psychiatric Institute (Atlanta)
(404) 436-0091   Ext. 777

Candler General Hospital (Savannah)
(912) 356-6290

Central Health Service (Atlanta)
(404) 644-6536

Charter Medical Corporation (Statewide)
(800) 334-5392

Charter Northside Hospital (Savannah)
(912) 757-5993

Cobb Hospital and Medical Center (Atlanta)
(404) 732-4050

De Kalb Medical Center (Atlanta)
(404) 501-5013

Eggleston Children's Hospital at Emory University
(Atlanta)
(404) 325-6477

Georgia Baptist Medical Center (Atlanta)
(404) 653-4066

Georgia Society of Hospital Pharmacists (Atlanta)
(404) 508-1717

Grady Health Systems (Atlanta)
(404) 616-JOBS

Gwinnett Hospital System (Atlanta)
(404) 995-4401

Hutcheson Medical Center (Fort Oglethorpe)
(706) 858-2144

Georgia

Kaiser Permanente (Atlanta)
(404) 365-7230

Kennestone Hospital (Marietta)
(404) 426-3170

Medical College of Georgia—School of Dentistry
(Augusta)
(706) 721-2900

Memorial Medical Center (Savannah)
(912) 350-8120

Newton General Hospital (Covington)
(404) 522-6188

North Fulton Regional Hospital (Atlanta)
(404) 751-2658

Northside Hospital (Atlanta)
(404) 303-3305

R. T. Jones Memorial Hospital (Atlanta)
(404) 720-5102

St. Francis Hospital (Columbus)
(706) 596-4090

St. Joseph's Hospital (Atlanta)
(404) 851-7048

St. Joseph's Hospital (Augusta)
(706) 596-7465

St. Joseph's Hospital (Savannah)
(912) 927-5156

Scottish Rite Children's Medical Center (Atlanta)
(404) 250-2184 (Nonnursing)

Scottish Rite Children's Medical Center (Atlanta)
(404) 250-2183 (Nursing)

Southeastern Health Services (Atlanta)
(404) 431-5348

South Fulton Medical Center (Atlanta)
(404) 305-4735

University Hospital (Athens)
(706) 826-8933

Wesley Homes, Incorporated (Atlanta)
(404) 728-6280

Miscellaneous

American Family Life Assurance Company (Augusta)
(706) 596-5959

American Telephone & Telegraph (Statewide)
(404) 810-7001 (Metro Atlanta)

American Telephone & Telegraph (Statewide)
(800) 562-7288

American Telephone & Telegraph (Statewide)
(800) 562-7665 (TDD)

American Telephone & Telegraph Tridom (Marietta)
(404) 514-3411

Atlanta Gaslight Company (Atlanta)
(404) 584-4705

Atlanta Journal and Constitution (Atlanta)
(404) 526-5092

Bell South (Atlanta)
(404) 391-3294

Bell South Advertising and Publishing (Atlanta)
(404) 491-1747

Brown and Williamson Tobacco Company (Macon)
(912) 749-8675

Georgia

Confederation Life Insurance (Atlanta)
(404) 859-3750

Creditor Resources, Incorporated (Atlanta)
(404) 257-8301

Digital Communications Association (Atlanta)
(404) 442-4010

Equifax (Atlanta)
(404) 612-2558

Equifax (Atlanta)
(404) 740-4635 (May contain same information found in previous entry)

Equifax (Atlanta)
(404) 885-8550 (May contain same information found in previous entries)

GEICO Insurance Company (Macon)
(912) 744-5092

General Mills (Atlanta)
(404) 784-2500

General Motors (Doraville)
(404) 455-5100

Georgia Power Company (Athens)
(706) 357-6630

Georgia Power Company (Macon)
(912) 784-5995

Gerber Alley (Norcross)
(404) 441-7793   Ext. 2893

GTE (Atlanta)
(404) 395-8500

Gulf Stream Aerospace Corporation (Savannah)
(912) 964-3130

Hewlett-Packard Company (Atlanta)
(404) 916-8899

International Business Machines (Atlanta)
(404) 877-5200

Jackson Electric Membership Corporation (Atlanta)
(404) 822-3280

John H. Harland Company (Atlanta)
(404) 593-5392 (Clerical)

John H. Harland Company (Atlanta)
(404) 593-5391 (Professional)

John H. Harland Company (Atlanta)
(404) 593-5395 (Production)

John H. Harland Company (Atlanta)
(404) 981-1270 (Production)

Lockheed Aeronautical Systems (Atlanta)
(404) 494-5000

Macon/Bibb County Water and Sewage Authority
(Macon)
(912) 741-2633

Macon Telegraph (Macon)
(912) 744-4353

Macy's (Augusta)
(706) 731-5800

MCI Telecommunications Corporation (Atlanta)
(404) 668-6864

Metro Area Rapid Transit Association (Atlanta)
(404) 848-5231

National Data Corporation (Atlanta)
(404) 728-2030

Georgia

National Linen Service (Atlanta)
(404) 853-6112

Northern Telecom Incorporated (Atlanta)
(404) 840-5501

Older Workers' Jobline (Atlanta)
(404) 364-2557

Pepsi-Cola (Atlanta)
(404) 352-7622

Quik Trip (Atlanta)
(800) 324-0935

Rockwell International Corporation (Atlanta)
(404) 476-6474

Rollins Incorporated (Atlanta)
(404) 888-2125

Six Flags Over Georgia (Atlanta)
(404) 739-3410

The Southern Company (Atlanta)
(404) 668-3464

Sprint International (Atlanta)
(404) 859-8398

Total System Services, Incorporated (Columbus)
(706) 649-4600

Trane Company (Macon)
(912) 788-5723

Travelers Insurance Company (Atlanta)
(404) 246-7056

Union Camp (Savannah)
(912) 238-6099

United Parcel Service (Atlanta)
 (404) 913-6800

Zoo Atlanta (Atlanta)
 (404) 624-5600   Ext. 4

Hawaii

Cities

Honolulu (City and County)
(808) 523-4303

State

State of Hawaii (Oahu)
(808) 587-0977

State of Hawaii (Oahu)
(808) 587-1148 (TDD)

State of Hawaii (Oahu)
(800) 468-4644   Inter-island Ext. 70977 (Mon. through Fri., 7:45 A.M. to 4:30 P.M.)

Federal

Fort Shafter (Oahu)
(808) 438-9301

Fort Shafter (Oahu)
(808) 438-6806 (May contain same information found in previous entry)

Hickam Air Force Base (Oahu)
(808) 449-6733

Kaneohe Marine Corps Air Station (Oahu)
(808) 254-4179

Federal Job Information Center (Statewide)
(808) 541-2791

Federal Job Information Center (Statewide)
(808) 541-2780 (May contain same information found in previous entry)

Office of Personnel Management (Statewide)
(808) 541-2784

Pearl Harbor (Oahu)
(808) 471-0850

United States Postal Service (Statewide)
(808) 423-3690

Banks

First Hawaiian Bank (Oahu)
(808) 525-5627

Pioneer Federal Savings Bank (Oahu)
(808) 522-6701

Education

Kamehameha Schools/Bishop Estates (Oahu)
(808) 842-8686

Hotels

ITT Sheraton Hotels (Oahu)
(808) 924-5294

Kapalua Bay Hotel and Villas (Maui)
(808) 669-4626

Outrigger Hotels (Oahu)
(808) 921-6777

Pacific Beach Hotels (Oahu)
(808) 921-6110

Medical/Hospitals

Kaiser Permanente Medical Center (Oahu)
(808) 539-5569

Queen's Medical Center (Oahu)
(808) 547-5573

Straub Clinic and Hospital (Oahu)
(808) 948-0505

Straub Clinic and Hospital (Oahu)
(808) 547-4473 (May contain same information found in previous entry)

Straub Clinic and Hospital (Oahu)
(808) 547-4355 (May contain same information found in previous entries)

Miscellaneous

American Telephone & Telegraph (Oahu)
(800) 562-7288

American Telephone & Telegraph (Oahu)
(800) 562-7665 (TDD)

City Mill (Oahu)
(808) 929-5840

Crazy Shirts, Incorporated (Oahu)
(808) 486-6312

Roberts Hawaii (Oahu)
(808) 539-9406

Safeway (Statewide)
(800) 255-0812 (Within Hawaii)

Servco Pacific (Statewide)
(808) 531-5515

Idaho

Cities

Boise
 (208) 384-3855

Counties

ADA (Boise)
 (208) 383-4429 (General)

ADA (Boise)
 (208) 377-6707 (Sheriff)

Boise (Idaho City)
 (208) 392-6636

State

Board of Corrections (Boise)
 (208) 334-2318

Department of Agriculture (Boise)
 (209) 334-3457

Department of Education (Boise)
 (208) 334-2203

Idaho Job Service (Boise)
 (208) 334-2626 (Clerical)

Idaho Job Service (Boise)
 (208) 334-2627 (Industrial/Service)

Idaho

Idaho Job Service (Boise)
(208) 334-2625 (Professional)

Idaho Personnel Commission (Statewide)
(208) 334-2568

State of Idaho (Twin Falls)
(208) 334-7021

Federal

Bureau of Reclamation (Boise)
(208) 334-9068

Mountain Home Air Force Base (Mountain Home)
(208) 828-2765

Banks

First Interstate Bank (Boise)
(208) 389-4136

First Security Bank (Boise)
(208) 338-2453

West One Bancorp (Boise)
(208) 383-5400

Education

University of Idaho (Moscow)
(208) 885-5702

Medical/Hospitals

Cassia Memorial Hospital and Medical Center (Burley)
(208) 678-6422

Hillcrest Rehabilatation Care Center (Boise)
(208) 245-4464

Magic Valley Regional Medical Center (Twin Falls)
 (208) 737-2775

St. Alphonsus Regional Medical Center (Boise)
 (208) 378-2106

St. Luke's Regional Medical Center (Boise)
 (208) 386-2465

West Valley Medical Center (Caldwell)
 (208) 455-3828

Miscellaneous

Albertson's Incorporated (Boise)
 (208) 385-6422

Boise Cascade Corporation (Boise)
 (208) 384-4900

Hewlett-Packard Company (Boise)
 (208) 323-5200

Idaho Power Company (Boise)
 (208) 383-2950

Micron Technology, Inc. (Boise)
 (208) 368-4141

MCI (Statewide)
 (800) 288-9378

Simplot Company (Boise)
 (208) 384-8002

Illinois

Cities

Chicago
  (312) 744-1369

Springfield
  (217) 789-2440

Federal

Federal Job Information Center (Illinois)
  (312) 353-6192

Federal Job Information Center (Wisconsin)
  (312) 353-6189

Rock Island Arsenal (Rock Island)
  (309) 782-2214

Scott Air Force Base (Belleville)
  (618) 256-6520

Banks

First Chicago (Chicago)
  (312) 407-JOBS

Harris Bank (Chicago)
  (312) 461-6900

Education

DePaul University (Chicago)
  (312) 855-8153

Southern Illinois University (Carbondale)
(618) 536-2116

Southern Illinois University (Edwardsville)
(618) 692-2420

Southern Illinois University Medical School
(Springfield)
(217) 782-8446

Southern Illinois University Medical School (Springfield)
(217) 782-5692 (May contain same information found
in previous entry)

Medical/Hospitals

Chicago Memorial Hospital (Chicago)
(312) 880-4998

Illini Hospital (Silvis)
(309) 792-7077

Rush-Presbyterian–St. Luke's Medical Center (Chicago)
(312) 942-3456

St. John's Hospital (Springfield)
(217) 525-5600

Trinity Medical Center (Moline)
(309) 757-2243

Miscellaneous

Abbott Laboratories (Abbott Park)
(708) 938-6295

American Airlines (Chicago)
(312) 686-4212

Amtrak (Chicago)
(312) 930-4293

Illinois

Cellular One (Peoria)
(708) 303-3444

Chicago and Northwestern Transportation Company
(Chicago)
(312) 559-6746

Chicago Park District (Chicago)
(312) 294-2410

Commonwealth Edison (Chicago)
(312) 509-3261 (North)

Commonwealth Edison (Chicago)
(312) 838-4218 (South)

Commonwealth Edison (Joliet)
(815) 727-5613

Commonwealth Edison (Libertyville)
(708) 816-5596

Commonwealth Edison (Lombard)
(708) 691-4602

Illinois Bell Telephone (Statewide)
(800) 942-9240 (Calls Within Illinois Only)

Illinois Bell Telephone (Statewide)
(800) 624-8291 (Outside Illinois)

Library Job Line of Illinois (Nationwide)
(312) 828-0930

McDonalds Corporation (Oak Brook)
(709) 575-5490

Montgomery Elevator (Moline)
(309) 757-5693

Quaker Oats (Chicago)
(312) 222-7744

Shell Oil Company (Alton)
(618) 254-8840

United Airlines (Chicago)
(708) 952-4094

U.S. Messenger (Chicago)
(312) 326-6540

Indiana

Cities

Fort Wayne
 (219) 427-1186

State

State of Indiana (Statewide)
 (317) 232-3101

State of Indiana (Statewide)
 (317) 232-4555 (TDD)

Federal

Fort Benjamin Harrison (Indianapolis)
 (317) 542-2454

Fort Benjamin Harrison (Indianapolis)
 (317) 542-2445 (TDD)

Naval Air Warfare Center—Aircraft Division
 (Indianapolis)
 (317) 353-7948

Office of Personnel Management (Statewide)
 (317) 226-7161

Office of Personnel Management (Statewide)
 (317) 426-6022 (TDD)

United States Postal Service (Indianapolis)
 (317) 464-6028

Banks

Bank One (Indianapolis)
  (317) 321-7987

First Indiana Bank (Indianapolis)
  (317) 269-1650

INB National Bank (Indianapolis)
  (317) 266-7788

National City Bank (Indianapolis)
  (317) 267-7700

Peoples Bank and Trust (Indianapolis)
  (317) 237-8132

Trust Indiana Bank (Indianapolis)
  (317) 269-1650

Education

Indiana University (Bloomington)
  (812) 855-9102

Indiana University (Fort Wayne)
  (219) 481-6971

Indiana University (Indianapolis)
  (317) 274-2255

Purdue University (West Lafayette)
  (317) 494-7417 (Administrative/Professional)

Purdue University (West Lafayette)
  (317) 494-7418 (Clerical)

Purdue University (West Lafayette)
  (317) 494-7419 (Service)

Purdue University (West Lafayette)
  (317) 494-6957 (Technical/Scientific)

Indiana

University of Notre Dame (South Bend)
(219) 631-4663 (Office, Clerical, Service, Library, Maintenance Personnel)

University of Notre Dame (South Bend)
(219) 631-4653 (Professional, Administrative, Technical)

Hotels

Resort Condominiums International (Indianapolis)
(317) 871-9724

Westin Hotel (Indianapolis)
(317) 231-3996

Westin Hotel (Indianapolis)
(317) 231-3948 (TDD)

Medical/Hospitals

Community Hospital (Indianapolis)
(317) 355-5599 (East)

Community Hospital (Indianapolis)
(317) 841-5366 (North)

Community Hospital (Indianapolis)
(317) 887-7562 (South)

Eli Lilly and Company (Indianapolis)
(317) 276-7472

Hendricks Community Hospital (Danville)
(317) 745-3712

Iupui Hospitals (Indianapolis)
(317) 274-2255

Methodist Hospital (Indianapolis)
(317) 290-7888

Metrohealth (Indianapolis)
(317) 571-5339

Midwest Medical Center (Indianapolis)
(317) 927-2231

St. Francis Hospital (Indianapolis)
(317) 783-8333

St. Mary's Medical Center (Evansville)
(812) 479-4473

St. Vincent Hospital (Indianapolis)
(317) 879-1141 (General)

St. Vincent Hospital (Indianapolis)
(317) 871-6543 (Nursing)

St. Vincent Hospital (Indianapolis)
(317) 870-8450 (TDD)

Union Hospital (Terre Haute)
(812) 238-7200

Welborn Clinic (Evansville)
(812) 426-9331

Westview Hospital (Indianapolis)
(317) 924-1071

Miscellaneous

American General Finance Corporation (Evansville)
(812) 468-5600

Boehringer Mannheim Corporation (Indianapolis)
(317) 845-7035

Citizens Gas and Coke Utility (Indianapolis)
(317) 927-4637

CONSECO (Indianapolis)
(317) 571-3333

Indiana

Education Financial Services (Indianapolis)
(317) 469-2184

Golden Rule Insurance Company (Indianapolis)
(317) 291-1859

Indiana Bell Telephone Company (Indianapolis)
(317) 556-4222

Indiana Michigan Power Company (Fort Wayne)
(219) 425-2345

Indianapolis Power and Light Company (Indianapolis)
(317) 261-8515

Manpower Temporary Services (Indianapolis)
(317) 637-7757

Merchants National Corporation (Indianapolis)
(317) 267-7700

Meridian Insurance Company (Indianapolis)
(317) 927-8180

Prentice Hall Computer Publishing Company
(Indianapolis)
(317) 571-3266

PSI Energy Inc. (Plainfield)
(317) 838-2838

Thomson Consumer Electronics (Indianapolis)
(317) 267-1840

Iowa

Cities

Cedar Rapids
 (319) 363-7000

Des Moines
 (515) 284-4115

State

Iowa Department of Personnel (Des Moines)
 (515) 281-5820

Federal

Federal Job Information Center (Iowa City)
 (816) 426-7757

United States Post Office (Des Moines)
 (515) 283-7506

Education

Drake University (Des Moines)
 (515) 271-4144

Iowa State University (Ames)
 (515) 294-0146 (Clerical)

Iowa State University (Ames)
 (515) 294-0147 (Security/Technical Skilled)

University of Iowa (Iowa City)
(319) 335-2682 (Clerical)

University of Iowa (Iowa City)
(319) 335-2686 (Professional)

University of Iowa (Iowa City)
(319) 335-2684 (Service)

University of Iowa (Iowa City)
(319) 335-2685 (Technical/Craft/Trade)

Medical/Hospitals

Mercy Hospital Medical Center (Davenport)
(319) 383-1260

Mercy Hospital Medical Center (Des Moines)
(515) 247-3105

Miscellaneous

Alcoa (Davenport)
(319) 359-2832

Pioneer Hi-Bred International, Inc. (Des Moines)
(515) 270-4000

Quik Trip (Statewide)
(800) 325-0935

Kansas

Cities

Kansas City
 (913) 573-5688

Kansas City
 (913) 573-2613 (May contain same information found in previous entry)

Overland Park
 (913) 381-5252

Topeka
 (913) 296-2208

Topeka
 (913) 271-1313 (May contain same information found in previous entry)

Wichita
 (316) 268-4537

Counties

Johnson (Olathe)
 (913) 780-2929

State

Kansas Division of Personnel (Topeka)
 (913) 296-2208

Kansas

Federal

Federal Job Information Center (Wichita)
(316) 269-0552

Fort Leavenworth (Leavenworth)
(913) 684-5533

Fort Riley (Junction City)
(913) 239-6066

McConnell Air Force Base (Wichita)
(316) 652-6104

Banks

Union National Bank (Wichita)
(316) 261-4924

U.S. Central Credit Union (Kansas City)
(913) 661-5321

Hotels

Marriott (Overland Park)
(913) 451-0259

Medical/Hospitals

Bethany Medical Center (Kansas City)
(913) 281-4475

Kaiser Permanente (Kansas City)
(913) 967-4701

Kansas University Medical Center (Kansas City)
(913) 588-5122

Overland Park Regional Medical Center (Overland Park)
(913) 541-5999

St. Francis Regional Medical Center (Wichita)
(316) 268-5191

St. Francis Regional Medical Center (Wichita)
(800) 362-0070   (Ask for Jobline)

St. Joseph Medical Center (Wichita)
(316) 689-6460

Stormont-Vail Regional Medical Center (Topeka)
(913) 354-5579

University of Kansas Medical Center (Topeka)
(913) 296-2208

Miscellaneous

Beech Aircraft Corporation (Wichita)
(316) 676-8435

Boeing (Wichita)
(316) 529-5040

Century Computer Consultants (Kansas City)
(913) 383-7575

Cessna Aircraft Company (Wichita)
(316) 941-6155

Coca-Cola Bottling Company of Mid-America (Kansas City)
(913) 599-9360

Learjet Inc. (Wichita)
(316) 946-2562

Manpower Temporary Services (Wichita)
(316) 942-9675

Quik Trip (Statewide)
(800) 324-0935

Kentucky

Cities

Louisville
 (502) 625-3355

Counties

Jefferson
 (502) 625-6182

Federal

Fort Knox (Radcliffe)
 (502) 624-5520

Office of Personnel Management (Statewide)
 (513) 225-2720

United States Internal Revenue Service (Covington)
 (606) 292-5304

United States Postal Service (Louisville)
 (502) 454-1625

Banks

First Kentucky National Corporation (Louisville)
 (502) 581-6453

Liberty National Bank (Louisville)
 (502) 566-1629

Education

Jefferson County Board of Education (Louisville)
(502) 473-3185

University of Kentucky (Lexington)
(606) 257-3841

University of Louisville (Louisville)
(502) 588-5627

Watterson College (Louisville)
(502) 491-9675

Medical/Hospitals

Alliant Medical Pavilion/Kosair Children's Hospital/Norton Memorial Hospital (Louisville)
(502) 629-8498

Alliant Medical Pavilion/Kosair Children's Hospital/Norton Memorial Hospital (Louisville)
(800) 789-JOBS (Press 1)

Humana (Audubon)
(502) 636-7350

Humana (Louisville)
(502) 580-3450 (Corporate)

Humana (Louisville)
(502) 562-3155 (University of Louisville)

St. Elizabeth Medical Center (Covington)
(606) 292-4480

Veteran's Administration Medical Center (Louisville)
(502) 894-6176

Kentucky

Miscellaneous

Access Computer Career Jobline (Louisville)
(502) 329-0222

Ashland Oil Inc. (Russell)
(606) 329-4328

Brown-Foreman Corp. (Louisville)
(502) 774-7191

Courier Journal/Louisville Times (Louisville)
(502) 582-7000

General Electric (Louisville)
(502) 452-0006

Houch Career Consultants (Louisville)
(502) 329-0601

Independent Order of Foresters (Louisville)
(502) 429-6846

Lantech, Inc. (Louisville)
(502) 267-4288   Ext. 597

National Processing Company (Louisville)
(502) 364-2394

Philip Morris USA (Louisville)
(502) 495-7585

Louisiana

Federal

Federal Job Information Center (New Orleans)
(504) 589-2764

Banks

Commercial National Bank (Shreveport)
(318) 227-6841

Hibernia National Bank (Baton Rouge)
(504) 381-2353

Hibernia National Bank (New Orleans)
(504) 586-5518

Premier Bank (Baton Rouge)
(504) 332-3512

Whitney National Bank (New Orleans)
(504) 586-3482

Education

Louisiana State University (Baton Rouge)
(504) 388-1101 (Classified)

Louisiana State University (Baton Rouge)
(504) 388-1201 (Unclassified/Academic)

Tulane University (New Orleans)
(504) 865-5627

Medical/Hospitals

East Jefferson General Hospital (Metairie)
(504) 454-4188

Meadowcrest Hospital (New Orleans)
(504) 391-5145

Schumpert Medical Center (Shreveport)
(318) 227-6841

West Jefferson Medical Center (Marrero)
(504) 349-1175

Miscellaneous

Bell South Cellular (Statewide)
(800) 669-0136

Central Louisiana Electric Company (Pineville)
(318) 484-7628

Ciba-Geigy Corporation (Baton Rouge)
(504) 642-1750

Martin Marietta Corporation (New Orleans)
(504) 257-4940

South Central Bell Telephone Company (New Orleans)
(504) 865-5627

Maine

Federal

Federal Job Information Center (Boston)
  (617) 565-5900

Miscellaneous

American Telephone & Telegraph (Statewide)
  (800) 858-5417

New England Library Association (Statewide)
  (617) 738-3148

Maryland

Cities

Rockville
 (301) 309-3273

Counties

Baltimore (Baltimore)
 (410) 887-5625

Carroll (Westminster)
 (410) 857-2020

Hartford (Bel Air)
 (410) 638-4473

Howard (Ellicott City)
 (410) 313-2900   Ext. 9220 (Clerical)

Howard (Ellicott City)
 (410) 313-2900   Ext. 9221 (Other)

Prince George (Landover)
 (301) 952-3408

State

Alcohol, Drug Abuse/Mental Health (Rockville)
 (301) 443-2282

Maryland National Capitol Park and Planning Commission (Hyattsville)
 (301) 927-5101   Ext. 8888

Maryland State Government (Baltimore)
(410) 333-5044

Federal

Agriculture Research Service (Greenbelt)
(301) 344-2288

Andrews Air Force Base (Capitol Heights)
(301) 988-8431

Coast Guard Yard (Curtis Bay)
(410) 677-4473

Federal Job Information Center (Baltimore)
(410) 962-3822

Fort Detrick (Fort Detrick)
(301) 619-2783

Fort Meade (Baltimore)
(410) 677-4473

Fort Ritchie (Silver Springs)
(301) 878-5264

Health Resources and Services (Rockville)
(301) 443-1230

Indian Health Services (Rockville)
(301) 443-6520

NASA Goddard Space Flight Center (Greenbelt)
(301) 286-5326

National Institute of Standards and Technology
(Gaithersburg)
(301) 926-4851

National Institutes of Health (Laurel)
(301) 496-2403

Maryland

Office of the Assistant Secretary of Health (Rockville)
(301) 443-1986

Patuxent River Naval Air Station (Patuxent River)
(301) 863-4801

United States Bureau of Census (Suitland)
(301) 763-7662

United States Bureau of Census (Suitland)
(301) 763-5537 (May contain same information found in previous entry)

United States Bureau of Census (Suitland)
(301) 763-6064   Ext. 3 (May contain same information found in previous entries)

United States Food and Drug Administration (Rockville)
(301) 443-1969

United States Naval Academy (Annapolis)
(410) 267-3821

Banks

First National Bank of Maryland (Baltimore)
(410) 347-6562

Loyola Federal (Baltimore)
(410) 332-2020

Provident Bank of Maryland (Baltimore)
(410) 281-7263

Education

Baltimore Public Schools (Baltimore)
(410) 887-4080

Johns Hopkins University (Baltimore)
(410) 955-3025 (Credit Union)

Johns Hopkins University (Baltimore)
(410) 955-2115 (School of Medicine)

Johns Hopkins University (Baltimore)
(410) 955-3025 (School of Nursing)

Montgomery College (Rockville)
(301) 279-5374 (Faculty)

Montgomery College (Rockville)
(301) 279-5373 (Staff)

Montgomery County Public Schools (Rockville)
(301) 279-3973

University of Maryland (Baltimore)
(410) 328-5562

University of Maryland (College Park)
(301) 405-5677

Hotels

Holiday Inn Crown Plaza (Rockville)
(301) 468-6470

Marriott Hotel (Baltimore)
(410) 637-5514

Marriott Hotel (Bethesda)
(301) 380-1202

Medical/Hospitals

Franklin Square Hospital Group (Baltimore)
(410) 682-8200

Greater Baltimore Medical Center (Baltimore)
(410) 828-3222

Greater Laurel-Beltsville Hospital (Laurel)
(301) 497-7909

Maryland

Holy Cross Hospital (Silver Springs)
(301) 538-2235

Maryland Medical Laboratories (Baltimore)
(410) 536-1445

Mercy Medical Center (Baltimore)
(410) 332-9414 (General)

Mercy Medical Center (Baltimore)
(410) 332-9399 (Housekeeping)

Mercy Medical Center (Baltimore)
(410) 332-9162 (Nursing)

Montgomery General Hospital (Olney)
(301) 774-8787

Prince George's Hospital Center (Hyattsville)
(301) 618-2261

Suburban Hospital (Bethesda)
(301) 530-3131

University of Maryland Medical System (Baltimore)
(410) 328-JOBS

Washington Adventist Hospital (Silver Springs)
(301) 891-6096

Miscellaneous

Alex Brown and Sons Inc. (Baltimore)
(410) 783-5350

Baltimore Gas and Electric Company (Baltimore)
(410) 234-7778

Baltimore Gas and Electric Company (Baltimore)
(410) 234-5831 (May contain information found in previous entry)

Barc Job Line (Baltimore)
(410) 685-5760

Bell Atlantic Network Services (Baltimore)
(410) 727-1200

Bell Atlantic Network Services (Hyattsville)
(301) 454-0754

Bethlehem Steel Corporation (Baltimore)
(410) 388-7258

Chesapeake Directory Sales Company (Hyattsville)
(301) 306-1580

Chesapeake Human Resources Group (Baltimore)
(410) 825-5478

Computer Data Systems, Inc. (Hyattsville)
(301) 921-7199

Discovery Network (Bethesda)
(301) 986-0444   Ext. 87

District Photo, Inc. (Beltsville)
(301) 937-5627

Giant Food (Baltimore)
(410) 521-5004

Hechinger (Rockville)
(301) 312-5320

International Business Machines (Rockville)
(301) 640-5434

Maryland Library Association (Statewide)
(410) 685-5760

Maxima Corporation (Lanham)
(301) 306-7499

McCormick and Company Inc. (Sparks)
(410) 527-6969

Maryland

Metpath (Rockville)
(301) 340-9800

Mid-Atlantic Coca-Cola Bottling Company (Baltimore)
(410) 312-5320

Monumental Life Insurance Company (Baltimore)
(410) 385-5995

Procter & Gamble (Baltimore)
(410) 785-4600

Quest Systems, Inc. (Baltimore)
(410) 771-5522

Quest Systems, Inc. (Bethesda)
(301) 229-2200

Residential Services Corporation of America
(Frederick)
(800) JOB-0075

Shopper's Food Warehouse Corporation (Lanham)
(301) 306-8600

Tracor Applied Science, Inc. (Rockville)
(301) 279-4646

USF&G Corporation (Baltimore)
(410) 625-5500

Massachusetts

Federal

Federal Job Information Center (Boston)
  (617) 565-5900

Education

Northeastern University (Boston)
  (617) 437-5373

Miscellaneous

All America Financial (Worcester)
  (508) 855-2372

American Telephone & Telegraph (Statewide)
  (800) 858-5417

Avery Dennison Manufacturing Company
  (Framingham)
  (508) 383-5627

Excel Placement, Inc. (Boston)
  (617) 422-1597

New England Library Association (Statewide)
  (617) 738-3148

Norton Company (Worcester)
  (508) 795-4664

Massachusetts

Paul Revere Life Insurance Company (Worcester)
 (508) 831-3455

Systems and Computer Technology (SCT) (Boston)
 (800) 722-2344

Michigan

Cities

Detroit
 (313) 224-6928

State

State of Michigan (Detroit)
 (313) 876-5627

Federal

Federal Job Information Center (Detroit)
 (313) 226-6950

Banks

Manufacturers Bank Corporation (Detroit)
 (313) 222-4610

Education

Detroit Public Schools (Detroit)
 (313) 833-2097

Lansing Community College (Lansing)
 (517) 483-9753

Michigan State University (East Lansing)
 (517) 355-9518

Michigan

Michigan Technological University (Houghton)
(906) 487-2895

Northern Michigan University (Marquette)
(906) 227-2562

University of Michigan (Ann Arbor)
(313) 764-7292

Medical/Hospitals

Blodgett Memorial Medical Center (Grand Rapids)
(616) 774-7277

Catherine McAuley Health System (Ann Arbor)
(313) 572-4063

Community Mental Health Board (Lansing)
(517) 887-2178

Mary Free Bed Hospital (Grand Rapids)
(616) 242-9285

St. Lawrence Hospital (Lansing)
(517) 377-0321

Upjohn Company (Kalamazoo)
(616) 329-5550

Miscellaneous

General Dynamics (Sterling Heights)
(313) 825-4292

Michigan Bell Telephone Company (Detroit)
(313) 223-8150

Michigan Library Association (Statewide)
(517) 694-7440

Michigan National Corporation (Farmington Hills)
(313) 473-4328

Minnesota

Cities

Minneapolis
 (612) 673-2666

St. Paul
 (612) 298-4942

Counties

Hennepin (Minneapolis)
 (612) 348-4698

Ramsey (St. Paul)
 (612) 266-2666

Washington (Stillwater)
 (612) 430-6083

State

Minnesota Department of Employee Relations
 (St. Paul)
 (612) 296-2616

Minnesota Department of Employee Relations
 (St. Paul)
 (612) 282-2699 (TDD)

Federal

Federal Job Information Center (Minneapolis/St. Paul)
 (612) 725-3430

Banks

IDS Financial Corporation (Minneapolis)
(612) 671-5059

Norwest Bank (Minneapolis)
(612) 667-5627

Miscellaneous

International Multifoods Corporation (Minneapolis)
(612) 340-3923

Land O' Lakes Inc. (St. Paul)
(612) 481-2250

McGlynn's Bakery (Minneapolis)
(612) 574-2222 (Ask for Jobline, 8 A.M. to 5 P.M., Mon. through Fri., Central Time)

Minnegasco (Minneapolis)
(612) 342-4666 (Weekdays)

Minnesota Mutual Life Insurance (St. Paul)
(612) 298-7934

Northwestern National Life Insurance (Minneapolis)
(612) 342-3594

Mississippi

Cities

Jackson
  (601) 960-1003

Federal

Keesler Air Force Base (Biloxi)
  (601) 377-3742

Banks

Deposit Guaranty National Bank (Jackson)
  (601) 354-8183

Education

University of Mississippi (University)
  (601) 232-7666

Medical/Hospitals

River Oaks Hospital (Jackson)
  (601) 936-2200

Miscellaneous

American Telephone & Telegraph (Statewide)
  (800) 562-7288

Mississippi

American Telephone & Telegraph (Statewide)
 (800) 562-7665 (TDD)

Bell South (Statewide)
 (800) 669-0136

Missouri

Cities

Blue Springs
  (816) 228-0290

Kansas City
  (816) 274-1127

Independence
  (816) 836-7104

Counties

Jackson (Independence)
  (816) 881-3134

Jackson County Circuit Court (Independence)
  (816) 881-3470

St. Louis (Clayton)
  (314) 889-3665

State

Missouri Career Information Hotline
  (800) 392-2949 (Mon. through Fri., 10 A.M. to 5 P.M. —
  Tues. to 9 P.M.)

Federal

Central Administration Center (Kansas City)
  (816) 426-7463

Missouri

Farmers Home Administration (St. Louis)
 (314) 539-2830

Federal Job Information Center (Kansas City)
 (816) 466-5702

Federal Job Information Center (St. Louis)
 (314) 539-2285

Fort Leonard Wood (Waynesville)
 (314) 596-5627

General Services Administration (Kansas City)
 (816) 926-7804

United States Army Corps of Engineers (St. Louis)
 (314) 331-8550

United States Internal Revenue Service (Kansas City)
 (816) 926-5498

United States Postal Service (Springfield)
 (417) 864-0126

United States Postal Service (St. Louis)
 (314) 436-3855

Whiteman Air Force Base (Knob Noster)
 (816) 687-6488

Banks

Boatmen's National Bank (St. Louis)
 (314) 466-4473

Commerce Bank (Kansas City)
 (816) 234-2139

Commerce Bank (St. Louis)
 (314) 746-7382

Mark Twain Financial (St. Louis)
(314) 863-7577

Mercantile Bank (Kansas City)
(816) 871-2113

United Missouri Bank (St. Louis)
(314) 394-7700

Education

Kansas City Public Schools (Kansas City)
(816) 871-7703

Metropolitan Community College (Kansas City)
(816) 759-1200

St. Charles Community College (St. Charles)
(314) 922-8301

St. Louis Community College (St. Louis)
(314) 539-5200

St. Louis University (St. Louis)
(314) 658-2265

Southwest Missouri State University (Springfield)
(417) 836-4683

University of Missouri (Columbia)
(314) 882-8800

University of Missouri (Kansas City)
(816) 235-1627

University of Missouri (Rolla)
(314) 341-4242

University of Missouri (St. Louis)
(314) 553-5926

Washington University School of Medicine (St. Louis)
(314) 362-7195

Missouri

Webster University (St. Louis)
(314) 968-7114

Medical/Hospitals

Barnes Hospital (St. Louis)
(314) 362-0700

Blue Cross/Blue Shield (Kansas City)
(816) 395-2725

Cardinal Glennon Children's Hospital (St. Louis)
(314) 577-5300

Christian Hospital Northeast (St. Louis)
(314) 355-2500   Ext. 3400

Cox Medical Center (Springfield)
(417) 888-5525

Deaconess Medical Center Central Campus (St. Louis)
(314) 768-3900

Freeman Hospital (Joplin)
(417) 625-3736

Independence Regional Health Center (Independence)
(816) 836-6655

Jewish Hospital (St. Louis)
(314) 454-5525

Menorah Medical Center (Kansas City)
(816) 276-8828

Research Medical Center (Kansas City)
(816) 276-4433

St. Joseph Health Center (Kansas City)
(816) 942-4669

St. Joseph Hospital (St. Louis)
(314) 966-1551

St. Louis Children's Hospital (St. Louis)
(314) 454-6070

Trinity Lutheran Hospital (Kansas City)
(816) 751-2090

Truman Medical Center (Kansas City)
(816) 556-3183

University Hospital and Clinics (Columbia)
(314) 882-8500

Miscellaneous

American Telephone & Telegraph (Kansas City)
(816) 654-2008

American Telephone & Telegraph (Statewide)
(800) 562-7288

American Telephone & Telegraph (Statewide)
(800) 562-7665 (TDD)

Anheuser-Busch Companies (St. Louis)
(314) 577-2392 (General)

Anheuser-Busch Companies (St. Louis)
(314) 577-3871 (Plant)

Brown Group (St. Louis)
(314) 854-2434

Century Computer Consultants (Kansas City)
(816) 383-7575

Continental Baking Company (St. Louis)
(314) 982-1800

Edward D. Jones Company (St. Louis)
(314) 851-2000

Emerson Electric Company (St. Louis)
(314) 553-2000

Missouri

Esco Electronics (St. Louis)
(314) 553-2485

Eveready Battery Company (St. Louis)
(314) 539-2830

Mallinckrodt Inc. (Hazelwood)
(314) 895-7355

McDonnell Douglas Corporation (Hazelwood)
(314) 232-4222

McDonnell Douglas Corporation (Hazelwood)
(314) 233-1801 (May contain same information found in previous entry)

Missouri Library Association (Statewide)
(314) 442-6590

Monsanto Chemical Company (Creve Coeur)
(314) 694-2650 (General)

Monsanto Chemical Company (Creve Coeur)
(314) 694-3489 (Professional)

Protein Technology International (St. Louis)
(314) 982-4896

Quik Trip (Kansas City/St. Louis)
(800) 324-0935

Ralston Purina (St. Louis)
(314) 982-2962 (Corporate)

Ralston Purina (St. Louis)
(314) 982-2020 (Grocer Product)

Schnucks Super Markets (St. Louis)
(314) 344-9292

Southwestern Bell Corporation (St. Louis)
(314) 247-2696

Montana

Cities

Billings
 (406) 657-8441

Bozeman
 (406) 586-3321

Butte
 (406) 723-8262

Helena
 (406) 447-8444

Missoula
 (406) 523-4703

Counties

Glacier (Cut Bank)
 (406) 813-2743

Missoula (Missoula)
 (406) 721-5700

Yellowstone (Billings)
 (406) 248-8880   Ext. 1399

State

Department of Personnel (Helena)
 (406) 444-3871

Montana

Department of Transportation (Helena)
(406) 444-6040

Highway Patrol (Kalispell)
(406) 756-5937

Job Service (Anaconda)
(406) 563-7862

Job Service (Billings)
(406) 252-6546

Job Service (Bozeman)
(406) 585-9019

Job Service (Butte)
(406) 782-1662

Job Service (Great Falls)
(406) 791-7755

Job Service (Hamilton)
(406) 363-2726

Job Service (Helena)
(406) 721-7092

Job Service (Helena)
(406) 252-6546 (May contain same information found in previous entry)

Job Service (Livingston)
(406) 222-0533

Job Service (Polson)
(406) 883-3311

Federal

Federal Job Opportunities Center (Statewide)
(303) 969-7052

United States Forest Service (Dillon)
  (406) 683-4612 (Beaverhead National Forest)

United States Forest Service (Helena)
  (406) 449-5419 (Helena National Forest)

United States Forest Service (Missoula)
  (406) 329-3786 (Lolo National Forest)

United States Postal Service (Billings)
  (406) 657-5763

United States Postal Service (Missoula)
  (406) 329-2280

United States Postal Service (Missoula)
  (406) 329-2228 (May contain same information found in previous entry)

Banks

First Interstate Bank of Montana (Billings)
  (406) 255-5219

Education

Eastern Montana College (Billings)
  (406) 657-2116

Montana State University (Bozeman)
  (406) 994-3343

Montana Technological (Butte)
  (406) 496-4268

University of Montana (Missoula)
  (406) 243-6760

Medical/Hospitals

Blue Cross/Blue Shield (Helena)
  (800) 821-0264 (Within Montana)

Montana

Deaconess Medical Center (Billings)
  (406) 657-4600

St. Peter's Community Hospital (Helena)
  (406) 447-2545

St. Vincent Hospital (Billings)
  (406) 657-8766

Miscellaneous

Mountain States Library Association (Statewide)
  (605) 677-5757

Nebraska

Cities

Lincoln
 (402) 441-7736

Omaha
 (402) 444-5302

Counties

Douglas (Omaha)
 (402) 444-6270

Douglas (Omaha)
 (402) 444-4664 (TDD)

Lancaster (Lincoln)
 (402) 471-3607

State

Job Service (Lincoln)
 (402) 471-3607

State of Nebraska (Lincoln)
 (402) 471-2200

State of Nebraska (Lincoln)
 (402) 471-4697 (May contain same information found in previous entry)

Federal

National Park Service (Omaha)
 (402) 221-3434

Offutt Air Force Base (Bellevue)
 (402) 294-6229

United States Postal Service (Lincoln)
 (402) 473-1669

United States Postal Service (Omaha)
 (402) 348-2523

Banks

Commercial Federal Bank (Omaha)
 (402) 398-4216

Firstier Bank (Lincoln)
 (402) 434-1426

Firstier Bank (Omaha)
 (402) 348-6400

National Bank of Commerce Trusts and Savings
 (Lincoln)
 (402) 434-4700

Education

Creighton University (Omaha)
 (402) 280-2943

University of Nebraska (Lincoln)
 (402) 472-2303

University of Nebraska (Omaha)
 (402) 554-2959

Hotels

Marriott (Omaha)
 (402) 391-6400

Red Lion Hotel (Omaha)
 (402) 346-1250

Medical/Hospitals

Blue Cross/Blue Shield (Omaha)
 (402) 398-3707

Bryan Memorial Hospital (Lincoln)
 (402) 483-3696

Clarkson Hospital (Omaha)
 (402) 552-3110 (Nonnursing)

Clarkson Hospital (Omaha)
 (402) 486-7694 (Nursing)

Fabiths, Inc. (Lincoln)
 (402) 489-8697

Lincoln General Hospital (Lincoln)
 (402) 435-0092

Madonna Rehabilitation Hospital (Lincoln)
 (402) 483-9468

Midlands Community Hospital (Papillion)
 (402) 593-3278

St. Elizabeth's Community Hospital (Lincoln)
 (402) 486-7098

St. Joseph's Hospital (Omaha)
 (402) 449-4451

Smithkline Beecham (Lincoln)
 (402) 473-2660

Nebraska

Miscellaneous

A Help, Inc. (Omaha)
(402) 691-6915

American Life Insurance Corporation (Lincoln)
(402) 467-7199

Conagra Inc. (Omaha)
(402) 595-4499

Express Temporary and Permanent (Lincoln)
(402) 421-2100

Mountain Plains Library Association (Statewide)
(605) 677-5757

Mutual of Omaha Insurance Company (Omaha)
(402) 978-2040

Nebraska Furniture Mart (Omaha)
(402) 392-3231

Nebraska Library Commission (Statewide)
(402) 471-2045 (Outside Nebraska)

Nebraska Library Commission (Statewide)
(800) 742-7691 (Nebraska Only)

Omaha Public Power District (Omaha)
(402) 636-3046

Physician's Mutual Life Insurance Company (Omaha)
(402) 633-1004

WATS Telemarketing (Omaha)
(402) 397-JOBS

Nevada

Cities

Boulder City
 (702) 293-9430

Carson City
 (702) 687-4160

Henderson
 (702) 565-2318

Las Vegas
 (702) 229-6346

North Las Vegas
 (702) 642-9266

Reno
 (702) 334-2287

Counties

Clark (Las Vegas)
 (702) 455-3174

Douglas (Gardnerville)
 (702) 782-9824

Washoe (Reno)
 (702) 328-2091

State

Nevada State Jobline (Carson City)
 (702) 687-4160

Nevada

Nevada State Jobline (Las Vegas)
(702) 486-4020

Federal

Nellis Air Force Base (Las Vegas)
(702) 652-3464

Banks

First Interstate Bank of Nevada (Las Vegas)
(702) 791-6251

First Interstate Bank of Nevada (Reno)
(702) 334-5666

Primerit Bank (Las Vegas)
(702) 226-0466

Education

Washoe County School District (Reno)
(702) 348-0386

Hotels

Fremont Hotel (Las Vegas)
(702) 385-6250

Harrah's Hotel and Casino (Las Vegas)
(702) 369-5050

Imperial Palace (Las Vegas)
(702) 794-3191

Palace Station Hotel (Las Vegas)
(702) 253-2950

Medical/Hospitals

Desert Springs Hospital (Las Vegas)
(702) 369-7737

Desert Springs Hospital (Las Vegas)
(800) 872-9500

HCA Montvista Hospital (Las Vegas)
(702) 251-1226

St. Rose Dominican Hospital (Henderson)
(702) 564-4796

Sparks Family Hospital (Reno)
(702) 356-4044

Miscellaneous

Central Telephone of Nevada (Las Vegas)
(702) 877-7566

EG&G Inc. (Las Vegas)
(702) 295-0200

Las Vegas Valley Water District (Las Vegas)
(702) 258-3220

Mountain Plains Library Association (Statewide)
(605) 677-5757

Mountain Plains Library Association (Statewide)
(800) 356-7820 (Within Nevada)

Nevada Power Company (Las Vegas)
(702) 367-5200

Prime Cable (Las Vegas)
(702) 384-9260

Southwest Gas Corporation (Las Vegas)
(702) 876-7106

New Hampshire

Federal

Federal Job Information Center (Statewide)
(617) 565-5900

Pease Air Force Base (Newington)
(603) 430-0100

United States Postal Service (Manchester)
(603) 644-4065

Education

Daniel Webster College (Nashua)
(603) 883-3556

Daniel Webster College (Nashua)
(603) 595-9911 (May contain same information found in previous entry)

Dartmouth College (Hanover)
(603) 646-3328

Proctor Academy (Manchester)
(603) 735-6000

University of New Hampshire (Durham)
(603) 862-4473

University of New Hampshire (Lee)
(603) 868-1800

Medical/Hospitals

Blue Cross/Blue Shield (Concord)
  (603) 224-9511

Catholic Medical Center (Manchester)
  (603) 626-2550

Dartmouth-Hitchcock Medical Center (Lebanon)
  (800) JOB-DHMC
  (Press # sign and 5774) (Allied Health)
  (Press # sign and 5788) (Nursing Positions)

Roche Biomedical Laboratories (Manchester)
  (603) 624-4640

St. Joseph's Hospital and Trauma Center (Nashua)
  (603) 882-3000

Miscellaneous

American Telephone & Telegraph (Statewide)
  (800) 858-5417

New England Library Association (Statewide)
  (617) 738-3148

New Jersey

Education

Princeton University (Princeton)
 (609) 258-6130

Rutgers University (New Brunswick)
 (908) 932-3045

Hotels

Atlantic City Showboat Inc. (Atlantic City)
 (609) 343-4305

Bally's Grand Inc. (Atlantic City)
 (609) 340-2211

Harrah's Casino Hotel (Atlantic City)
 (609) 441-5681   Ext. 4

Medical/Hospitals

Monmouth Medical Center (Monmouth)
 (908) 870-5214

Miscellaneous

American Telephone & Telegraph (Statewide)
 (800) 858-5417

Atlantic City Electric Company (Pleasantville)
 (609) 625-5848

Continental Airlines (Newark)
 (201) 961-8505

New Jersey Bell Telephone Company (Newark)
 (201) 587-7564

New Jersey Library Association (Statewide)
 (609) 695-2121

New York Chapter, Special Libraries Association
 (Statewide)
 (212) 740-2007

Prudential Insurance Company (Newark)
 (201) 802-8494

New Mexico

Cities

Albuquerque
 (505) 768-4636

Federal

Cannon Air Force Base (Clovis)
 (505) 784-2401

Federal Job Information Center (Albuquerque)
 (505) 766-5583

Holloman Air Force Base (Alamogordo)
 (505) 479-7037

Office of Personnel Management (Albuquerque)
 (505) 766-1893

United States Postal Service (Albuquerque)
 (505) 848-3808

Education

New Mexico State University (Las Cruces)
 (505) 646-2006

University of New Mexico (Albuquerque)
 (505) 272-5627

Medical/Hospitals

Presbyterian Health Care System (Albuquerque)
(505) 841-1720

Miscellaneous

Ethicon Corporation (Albuquerque)
(505) 768-5239

General Mills (Albuquerque)
(505) 897-5400   Ext. 1

General Mills (Albuquerque)
(505) 845-4154   Ext. 1 (May contain same information found in previous entry)

Intel Corporation (Rio Rancho)
(505) 893-3998

New York

Cities

Manhattan
  (212) 566-8700

Federal

Federal Job Information Center (New York City)
  (212) 264-0422

United States Post Office (Syracuse)
  (315) 452-3438

Banks

Chase Bank (New York City)
  (800) JOB-LINE (Ask for Jobline)

Chase Bank (Rochester)
  (716) 258-5388

Education

Pace University (New York City)
  (212) 346-1893

Pratt Institute School of Library Science (New York City)
  (718) 636-3742

State University of New York (Albany)
  (518) 442-3151

State University of New York (Stony Brook)
(516) 632-9222

University of Rochester (Rochester)
(716) 275-2091

Hotels

Sheraton Centre Hotel and Tower (New York City)
(212) 841-6410

Medical/Hospitals

Blue Cross/Blue Shield of Central New York (Syracuse)
(315) 448-6735

Staten Island University Hospital (New York City/Staten Island)
(718) 226-9270

Visiting Nurse Service Home Care (New York City)
(212) 560-3342

Miscellaneous

American Telephone & Telegraph (Statewide)
(800) 858-5417

Avis Incorporated (Garden City)
(516) 222-3399

Bausch and Lomb, Inc. (Rochester)
(716) 338-6105

Club Med (New York City)
(212) 755-6458   Ext. 2

Daily News (New York City/Manhattan)
(212) 210-6300

New York

Eastman Kodak Company (Rochester)
(716) 724-4609   Ext. 1 (General)

Eastman Kodak Company (Rochester)
(716) 724-4609   Ext. 2 (Degreed Position)

Gannett Newspaper (Rochester)
(716) 258-2556

Gay Men's Health Crisis, Inc. (New York City)
(212) 337-1910

International Business Machines (White Plains)
(914) 288-5700

Key Services Corporation (Albany)
(518) 436-2533

National Fuel Gas Distribution Corporation (Buffalo)
(716) 857-7821

New York Chapter, Special Libraries Association
(Statewide)
(212) 740-2007

New York Library Association (Statewide)
(518) 432-6952 (General)

New York Library Association (Statewide)
(315) 443-2740 (School Library Media Specialists)

New York Library Association (Statewide)
(800) 232-6952 (Within New York)

New York Telephone (New York City)
(212) 395-2800   Ext. 2 (Management)

New York Telephone (New York City)
(212) 395-2800   Ext. 1 (Service/Technical)

New York Telephone (New York City)
(800) 698-5627 (Within New York State)

New York Times (New York City)
  (212) 556-1383

Pepsi-Cola Company (Somers)
  (914) 767-6300

North Carolina

Cities

Cary
 (919) 460-4905

Charlotte
 (704) 336-3968

Fayetteville
 (919) 433-1636

Greensboro
 (919) 373-2080

Raleigh
 (919) 890-3305

Counties

Forsyth (Winston-Salem)
 (919) 631-6333

New Hanover (Wilmington)
 (919) 341-7163

Wake (Durham)
 (919) 856-6115

Federal

Camp Lejeune Marine Base (Jacksonville)
 (919) 451-1621

Environmental Protection Agency (Research
  Triangle Park)
  (919) 541-3014

Federal Reserve Bank (Charlotte)
  (704) 358-2484

Fort Bragg (Fayetteville)
  (919) 396-5627

Pope Air Force Base (Fayetteville)
  (919) 394-2640

Banks

Wachovia Bank of North Carolina (Winston-Salem)
  (919) 770-5520

Education

Bowman Gray School of Medicine of Wake Forest
  University (Winston-Salem)
  (919) 716-3742

Duke University (Durham)
  (919) 684-8895 (Administrative)

Duke University (Durham)
  (919) 684-8896 (Clerical)

Duke University (Durham)
  (919) 684-8897 (Technical)

Guilford County Schools (Greensboro)
  (919) 271-0736

University of North Carolina (Chapel Hill)
  (919) 990-3000

University of North Carolina (Greensboro)
  (919) 334-5023

Medical/Hospitals

Blue Cross/Blue Shield of North Carolina (Durham)
(919) 490-2850

Durham County Hospital (Durham)
(919) 549-5001

Mercy Hospital (Charlotte)
(704) 379-5064

Moore Regional Hospital (Pinehurst)
(919) 215-1356

Orange-Person-Chatham Mental Health Center
(Chapel Hill)
(919) 967-0018

Presbyterian Hospital (Winston-Salem)
(704) 384-5350

Raleigh Community Hospital (Raleigh)
(919) 254-3653

Rex Hospital (Raleigh)
(919) 783-3157

University of North Carolina Hospitals (Chapel Hill)
(919) 966-1263

Wake Medical (Raleigh)
(919) 549-6974

Miscellaneous

Burroughs Wellcome (Research Triangle Park)
(919) 248-8347

GTE South Inc. (Durham)
(919) 471-6996

Manpower Temporary Service (Raleigh)
(919) 541-1618

News and Observer (Raleigh)
  (919) 549-5100   Ext. 5627

North Carolina Library Jobline (Statewide)
  (919) 733-6410

Seer Technologies (Raleigh)
  (919) 380-5350

Square D Company (Raleigh)
  (919) 266-8828

Underwriters Laboratories (Research Triangle Park)
  (919) 549-9626 (Administrative)

Underwriters Laboratories (Research Triangle Park)
  (919) 549-5227 (Technical)

North Dakota

State

North Dakota Job Service Jobline (Bismarck)
(701) 221-5094

North Dakota Job Service Jobline (Grand Forks)
(701) 795-3751

North Dakota Job Service Jobline (Williston)
(701) 857-7658

Federal

Federal Job Opportunities Center (North Dakota Only)
(800) 342-4781

Grand Forks Air Force Base (Grand Forks)
(701) 747-3436

Minot Air Force Base (Minot)
(701) 723-2811

Education

North Dakota State University (Fargo)
(701) 237-8273

Medical/Hospitals

Fargo Clinic–Meritcare (Fargo)
(701) 234-2341

Grand Forks Clinic (Grand Forks)
(701) 789-6225

St. Luke's Hospital–Meritcare (Fargo)
(701) 234-5136

United Hospital (Grand Forks)
(701) 780-5123

University of North Dakota School of Medicine
(Grand Forks)
(701) 777-3400

Miscellaneous

Mountain Plains Library Association (Statewide)
(800) 356-7820

Northern States Power Company (Minot)
(701) 839-8143

Taco John's (Fargo)
(701) 232-5662

US West (Fargo)
(800) 822-5853 (North Dakota Only)

US West (Fargo)
(701) 241-3274 (Outside North Dakota)

Ohio

Cities

Cincinnati
 (513) 352-2489

Federal

Office of Personnel Management (Cincinnati)
 (513) 225-2866

Office of Personnel Management (Cincinnati)
 (513) 225-2720 (May contain same information found in previous entry)

Wright-Patterson Air Force Base (Dayton)
 (513) 257-8311

Banks

Banc One Corporation (Columbus)
 (614) 248-0779

Fifth Third Bancorp (Cincinnati)
 (513) 579-JOBS

Huntington Bancshares Inc. (Columbus)
 (614) 463-4305

National City Bank (Columbus)
 (614) 463-6736

NBD Bank (Columbus)
 (614) 621-7048

Education

Columbus State Community College (Columbus)
(614) 227-5454

Dublin City Schools (Columbus)
(614) 764-5916

Ohio State University (Athens)
(614) 292-1212

Toledo City School District (Toledo)
(419) 729-8355

University of Toledo (Toledo)
(419) 537-2020

Medical/Hospitals

Abbott Ross Laboratories (Columbus)
(614) 624-7851

American Red Cross (Columbus)
(614) 251-1455

Children's Hospital (Columbus)
(614) 461-6881

Cleveland Clinic Foundation (Cleveland)
(216) 444-8971

Doctor's Hospital North (Columbus)
(614) 297-4367

Grandview Medical Center (Dayton)
(513) 226-2675

Jewish Hospital (Cincinnati)
(513) 569-2319

Medical College Hospitals (Toledo)
(419) 381-3040

Mercy Hospital (Toledo)
(419) 259-1312

Mount Carmel East Hospital (Columbus)
(614) 868-6731

Mount Carmel Medical Center (Columbus)
(614) 225-5767

Riverside Methodist Hospital (Columbus)
(614) 566-4748

St. Charles Hospital (Toledo)
(419) 698-7372

St. Luke Hospital (Toledo)
(419) 891-8050

Southview Hospital (Cincinnati)
(513) 226-2675

Miscellaneous

Battelle Memorial Institute (Columbus)
(614) 424-5627

BP America Inc. (Cleveland)
(216) 586-5662

Cleveland Area Metropolitan Library System
(Statewide)
(216) 921-4702

Comp-U-Card International (Columbus)
(614) 890-9032

Cuyahoga County Public Library (Cleveland)
(216) 749-9466

Judson Retirement Community (Cleveland)
(216) 791-2070

Nationwide Insurance (Columbus)
 (614) 249-5725

Nationwide Mutual Fire Insurance (Columbus)
 (614) 249-6419

Ohio Bell Telephone Company (Cleveland)
 (216) 822-2711

Ohio Bell Telephone Company (Columbus)
 (614) 223-8969

Pizza Hut (Cleveland)
 (216) 642-3276

Procter & Gamble (Cincinnati)
 (513) 983-2125

Sterling Software (Dublin)
 (614) 793-7232

Wendy's (Cincinnati)
 (513) 874-7904   Ext. 209

Oklahoma

Cities

Midwest City
 (405) 739-1236

Norman
 (405) 366-5321

Oklahoma City
 (405) 297-2419

Oklahoma City
 (405) 297-2549 (TDD)

Tulsa
 (918) 596-7444

State

Oklahoma Department of Libraries (Statewide)
 (405) 521-4202

State of Oklahoma (Oklahoma City)
 (405) 521-2171

Federal

Office of Personnel Management (Oklahoma City)
 (405) 231-4948

Tinker Air Force Base (Oklahoma City)
 (405) 739-3271

United States Army Corps of Engineers (Oklahoma City)
 (405) 599-6861

United States Postal Service (Norman)
(405) 366-4499 (Technical Training Center)

United States Postal Service (Oklahoma City)
(405) 278-6279

United States Postal Service (Tulsa)
(918) 599-6861

Vance Air Force Base (Enid)
(405) 237-2121

Banks

American Fidelity (Oklahoma City)
(405) 523-5627

Bank of Oklahoma (Tulsa)
(918) 588-6828

Liberty Bank and Trust Company (Tulsa)
(918) 586-5818

Education

Oklahoma State University (Stillwater)
(405) 744-7692

Oklahoma University College of Medicine (Tulsa)
(918) 838-4643

Oklahoma University College of Medicine (Tulsa)
(918) 838-4669 (TDD)

Oral Roberts University (Tulsa)
(918) 495-6035

University of Central Oklahoma (Edmond)
(405) 341-2980   Ext. 3089

University of Oklahoma (Norman)
(405) 325-4343 (Staff)

University of Oklahoma (Norman)
 (405) 325-2711 (Student)

Hotels

Sheraton Kensington (Tulsa)
 (918) 493-7000   Ext. 6564

Medical/Hospitals

Baptist Medical Center of Oklahoma (Oklahoma City)
 (405) 949-3101

Blue Cross/Blue Shield (Ada)
 (405) 332-8921

Blue Cross/Blue Shield (Enid)
 (405) 234-5938

Bone and Joint Hospital/McBride Clinic (Oklahoma City)
 (405) 272-9671   Ext. 369

Deaconess Hospital (Oklahoma City)
 (405) 949-6110

Edmond Regional Medical Center (Edmond)
 (405) 359-5511

Hillcrest Medical Center (Oklahoma City)
 (405) 680-2400

Mercy Medical Center (Oklahoma City)
 (405) 752-3721

Midwest City Regional Hospital (Midwest City)
 (405) 736-8106 (Nonnursing)

Midwest City Regional Hospital (Midwest City)
 (405) 736-8105 (Nursing)

Norman Regional Hospital (Norman)
(405) 360-8344

Oklahoma City Clinic (Oklahoma City)
(405) 271-3007

Presbyterian Hospital (Oklahoma City)
(405) 271-4712

St. Anthony's Hospital (Oklahoma City)
(405) 231-3700

St. Francis Hospital (Tulsa)
(918) 494-1700

St. John's Medical Center (Tulsa)
(918) 744-2303

St. John's Medical Center (Tulsa)
(918) 744-3330 (TDD)

South Community Hospital (Tulsa)
(918) 793-2233

Southwest Medical Center (Moore)
(405) 636-7050

Southwest Medical Center of Oklahoma (Oklahoma City)
(405) 531-4777

Springer Clinic (Tulsa)
(918) 747-8711

Tulsa Regional Medical Center (Tulsa)
(918) 582-4473

Miscellaneous

American Red Cross (Tulsa)
(918) 831-1233

Oklahoma

Daily Oklahoman (Oklahoma City)
(405) 475-3993

Dollar Rent-A-Car (Tulsa)
(918) 669-2380

Ford Motor Company (Tulsa)
(918) 254-5249

Hilti (Tulsa)
(918) 252-6001

Hitachi Computer Products (Norman)
(405) 329-7214

International Chemical Company (Tulsa)
(918) 496-7711

Metro Tech (Oklahoma City)
(405) 424-8324 (Ask for Job Line)

Mid-American Pipe Line (Tulsa)
(918) 586-7178

Mountain Plains Library Association (Statewide)
(605) 677-5757

Pentastar Services (Tulsa)
(918) 669-2380

Phillips 66 Company (Bartlesville)
(918) 661-5547

Public Service of Oklahoma (Tulsa)
(918) 599-3000

Quik Trip (Tulsa)
(800) 324-0935

Sun Company, Inc. (Tulsa)
(918) 586-6093

Oregon

Cities

Beaverton
 (503) 526-2299

Corvallis
 (503) 757-6955

Eugene
 (503) 687-5060

Gresham
 (503) 669-2309

Lake Oswego
 (503) 635-0256

Portland
 (503) 823-4573

Portland
 (503) 823-4352 (May contain same information found in previous entry)

Portland
 (503) 823-3520 (TDD)

Salem
 (503) 588-6107

Springfield
 (503) 726-3648

Tigard
(503) 624-9471

Counties

Benton (Corvallis)
(503) 757-6755

Clackamas (Oregon City)
(503) 655-8894

Curry (Gold Beach)
(503) 469-9513

Lane (Eugene)
(503) 687-4473

Lane (Eugene)
(503) 687-3995 (TDD)

Marion (Salem)
(503) 588-5589

Multnomah (Portland)
(503) 248-5035

Multnomah (Portland)
(503) 248-5170 (TDD)

Washington (Hillsboro)
(503) 648-8607

State

Oregon State Jobline (Eugene)
(503) 686-7652

Oregon State Jobline (Salem)
(503) 373-1199

Oregon State Jobline (Springfield)
(503) 726-2518

Federal

Federal Job Information Center (Portland)
(503) 326-3141

Office of Personnel Management (Portland)
(503) 249-0496

United States Department of Energy (Portland)
(503) 230-5784 (Current and Former Federal Employees Only)

United States Internal Revenue Service (Portland)
(503) 326-3688

United States Postal Service (Eugene)
(503) 341-3688

United States Postal Service (Portland)
(503) 294-2270

Banks

Bank of America (Portland)
(503) 275-1390

Far West Federal Bank (Portland)
(503) 323-6467

First Consumers National Bank (Portland)
(503) 520-8464

First Interstate Bank of Oregon (Portland)
(503) 778-8188

Key Bank of Oregon (Portland)
(503) 778-6077

U.S. Bancorp (Portland)
(503) 275-6401

Oregon

Washington Mutual Savings Bank (Portland)
(800) 952-0787 (Within Oregon/Washington only)

West One Bank (Oregon City)
(503) 225-1721

Education

Beaverton School District No. 48 (Beaverton)
(503) 591-4600

Chemeketa Community College (Salem)
(503) 399-5228

Clackamas Community College (Oregon City)
(503) 650-6655

Eugene School District No. 4J (Eugene)
(503) 687-3344

Gladstone School District No. 115 (Oregon City)
(503) 650-2573

Lake Oswego School District No. 7 (Lake Oswego)
(503) 635-0342

Lane Community College (Eugene)
(503) 726-6950

Lewis and Clark College (Portland)
(503) 768-7840

Linn-Benton Community College (Corvallis)
(503) 926-8800

Mount Hood Community College (Eugene)
(503) 667-7645

Multnomah Education Service (Portland)
(503) 257-1510

Oregon City School District No. 62 (Oregon City)
(503) 657-2465

Oregon Health Sciences University (Portland)
(503) 494-6478

Oregon State University (Corvallis)
(503) 737-0554

Portland Community College (Portland)
(503) 273-2826

Portland Public Schools (Portland)
(503) 280-5156

Portland School District No. 15 (Portland)
(503) 331-3102

Reed College (Portland)
(503) 777-7706

Salem-Keizer School District (Keizer)
(503) 399-3404 (Nonacademic)

Springfield School District No. 19 (Springfield)
(503) 726-9564

University of Oregon (Eugene)
(503) 346-3159

University of Portland (Portland)
(503) 283-7433 (Nonacademic)

Valley Community College (Dallas)
(503) 623-7324

Hotels

Hilton Hotel (Portland)
(503) 220-2560

Red Lion Hotels and Inns (Portland)
(503) 240-8598

Oregon

Medical/Hospitals

American Red Cross—Oregon Trail Chapter (Portland)
(503) 280-1454

American Telephone & Telegraph (Statewide)
(800) 423-6992

Blue Cross/Blue Shield of Oregon (Portland)
(503) 225-5402

Cottage Grove Hospital (Springfield)
(503) 942-0511   Ext. 325

Eastmoreland Hospital (Portland)
(503) 231-3485

Emanuel Hospital and Health Center (Portland)
(503) 280-4727

Eugene Clinic (Eugene)
(503) 687-6007

Good Samaritan Medical Center (Portland)
(503) 229-7061

Holladay Park Medical Center (Portland)
(503) 239-3116

Kaiser Permanente (Salem)
(503) 370-4866

McKenzie-Willamette Hospital (Springfield)
(503) 726-4501

Meridian Park Hospital (Portland)
(503) 692-2300

Merle West Medical Center (Klamath Falls)
(503) 883-6020

Mount Hood Medical Center (Portland)
(503) 661-9298

Multnomah County Medical Society Dental Placement
Service (Portland)
(503) 248-9855   Ext. 7700

PACC Health Plans (Clackamas)
(503) 652-5396

Portland Adventist Medical Center (Portland)
(503) 251-6295 (Nonnursing)

Portland Adventist Medical Center (Portland)
(503) 251-6195 (Nursing)

Providence Medical (Portland)
(503) 230-6010

Providence Medical (Portland)
(503) 230-6292 (May contain same information found in previous entry)

Providence-Milwaukie Hospital (Milwaukie)
(503) 652-8488

Sacred Heart General Hospital (Eugene)
(503) 686-6906 (Nonnursing)

Sacred Heart General Hospital (Eugene)
(503) 686-7205 (Nursing)

Sacred Heart General Hospital (Eugene)
(503) 686-8960 (TTY)

St. Vincent Medical Center (Portland)
(503) 291-2299

Salem Hospital (Salem)
(503) 370-5466

Salem Hospital (Salem)
(800) 825-5199 (May contain same information found in previous entry)

Oregon

Shriner's Hospital For Crippled Children (Portland)
  (503) 221-3459

Tuality Community Hospital (Hillsboro)
  (503) 681-1157

University Hospital Clinic (Portland)
  (503) 494-6478

Veterans Administration Medical Center (Portland)
  (503) 273-5249

Visiting Nurse Association (Portland)
  (503) 241-3489

Willamette Dental Group (Beaverton)
  (503) 671-9486

Woodland Park Hospital (Beaverton)
  (503) 257-5623

Miscellaneous

Avia Footware (Portland)
  (503) 520-5322

Boeing Portland (Portland)
  (503) 661-8318

Brookings Energy Facility (Portland)
  (503) 469-2677

Brookings Energy Facility (Portland)
  (800) 826-9801 (Within Oregon)

CBM Systems (Portland)
  (503) 657-7766

Cellular One (Portland)
  (503) 789-JOBS

Esco Foundry (Portland)
(503) 778-6564

Eugene Water and Electric Board (Eugene)
(503) 484-3769

Fred Meyer, Inc. (Portland)
(800) 401-JOBS

Freightliner Corporation (Portland)
(503) 735-8657 (Corporate)

Freightliner Corporation (Portland)
(503) 735-7284 (Parts/Manufacturing)

Freightliner Corporation (Portland)
(503) 735-7091 (Truck Manufacturing)

Fujitsu Microelectronics (Gresham)
(503) 669-6075

GTE (Beaverton)
(503) 526-2737

Gunderson, Inc. (Portland)
(503) 291-0639

Hewlett-Packard (Corvallis)
(503) 754-0919

Intel Corporation Systems Manufacturing (Hillsboro)
(503) 696-2580

Key Services Corporation (Tigard)
(503) 684-7311

KGW TV Channel 8 (Portland)
(503) 226-4590

McCaw Cellular Communications (Portland)
(503) 789-JOBS

Oregon

Mentor Graphics Corporation (Wilsonville)
(503) 685-1028

Metropolitan Service District (Portland)
(503) 220-1177

NEC America, Inc. (Hillsboro)
(503) 681-3593

Nike (Eugene)
(503) 644-4244

Northern Telecom, Inc. (Portland)
(800) 667-8437 (Press 9, 8 A.M. to 5 P.M., Mon. through Fri., Eastern Time)

Northwest Natural Gas Company (Portland)
(503) 220-2434

Oregon Cutting Systems—Division of Blount, Inc. (Beaverton)
(503) 653-4441

Oregon Library Association (Statewide)
(503) 585-2232

Oregon Museum of Science and Industry (Beaverton)
(503) 797-4665

The Oregonian (Portland)
(503) 294-4044

Owens-Illinois (Gresham)
(503) 251-9483

Pacific Northwest Library Association (Statewide)
(206) 543-2890

Pacificorp (Portland)
(503) 464-6848

Planar Systems (Beaverton)
(503) 690-6972

Port of Portland (Portland)
(503) 731-7480

Portland General Electric (Portland)
(503) 464-7441

Precision Cast Parts, Structural Division (Portland)
(503) 777-6077

Precision Interconnect (Portland)
(503) 684-4684

Safeway (Clackamas)
(503) 657-6400

SAIF Corporation (Salem)
(503) 373-8231

Standard Insurance (Portland)
(503) 248-2884

Tektronix Inc. (Wilsonville)
(503) 627-7737

Teufel Nursery, Inc. (Portland)
(503) 643-8706

TRI Met (Portland)
(503) 238-4840

United Grocers (Milwaukie)
(503) 652-7522

U.S. West (Statewide)
(503) 242-8593

Weyerhauser Paper Company (Springfield)
(503) 741-5910

Pennsylvania

Cities

Pittsburgh
  (412) 255-2388

Federal

Federal Job Information Center (Pittsburgh)
  (412) 644-2755

Education

Carnegie Mellon University (Pittsburgh)
  (412) 268-8545

Drexel University (Drexel)
  (215) 895-2562

Drexel University—College of Information (Drexel)
  (215) 895-1672

Penn State University (College Station)
  (814) 865-5627

Thomas Jefferson University (Philadelphia)
  (215) 955-8313

University of Pittsburgh (Pittsburgh)
  (412) 624-8040

Medical/Hospitals

Allegheny General Hospital (Pittsburgh)
 (412) 359-3201

Braddock Medical Center (Braddock)
 (412) 636-5394

McNeil Pharmaceuticals (Philadelphia)
 (215) 628-7840   Ext. 1

University of Pittsburgh Medical Center (Pittsburgh)
 (412) 647-3588

Miscellaneous

Boeing Helicopter (Philadelphia)
 (215) 591-2910

Equitable Resources Inc. (Pittsburgh)
 (412) 553-5733

Pennsylvania Library Association (Statewide)
 (717) 234-4646

Pennsylvania Library Association (Statewide)
 (800) 622-3113 (Within Pennsylvania only)

Peoples Natural Gas (Pittsburgh)
 (412) 497-6655

Philadelphia Electric Company (Philadelphia)
 (215) 841-4340

Systems and Computer Technology (SCT) (Malverne)
 (800) 722-2344

US Air (Pittsburgh)
 (412) 472-7693

Rhode Island

Education

Brown University (Providence)
  (401) 863-9675

Medical/Hospitals

St. Joseph Hospital (North Providence)
  (401) 456-3747

Miscellaneous

American Telephone & Telegraph (Statewide)
  (800) 858-5417

New England Library Association (Statewide)
  (617) 738-3148

New England Telephone Company (Statewide)
  (401) 727-9695 (Call collect)

South Carolina

Cities

Charleston
 (803) 720-3907

Charleston
 (803) 724-0694 (City and County Listings)

Columbia
 (803) 733-8478

Counties

Lexington (Lexington)
 (803) 359-8562

State

South Carolina Department of Corrections (Statewide)
 (803) 737-3616 (Administrative)

South Carolina Department of Corrections (Statewide)
 (803) 737-8524 (Professional)

South Carolina Department of Corrections (Statewide)
 (803) 737-8523 (Secretarial)

South Carolina Department of Corrections (Statewide)
 (803) 737-3618 (Trades)

South Carolina Department of Mental Health
 (Columbia)
 (803) 734-7674

Federal

Shaw Air Force Base (Sumter)
(803) 668-5384

Education

Clemson University (Clemson)
(803) 656-2228

University of South Carolina (Columbia)
(803) 777-2100 (Administrative)

University of South Carolina (Columbia)
(803) 777-6900 (Secretarial/Clerical)

University of South Carolina (Columbia)
(803) 777-8443 (Statewide Library Positions)

University of South Carolina (Columbia)
(803) 777-7728 (Technical)

Medical/Hospitals

Baptist Medical Center (Columbia)
(803) 771-5771

Roper Hospital (Charleston)
(803) 724-2472

Miscellaneous

Colonial Life and Accident Insurance Company
(Columbia)
(803) 750-0088

Educational Television Commission (Columbia)
(803) 737-3320

South Carolina Electric and Gas Company (Columbia)
  (803) 748-3001

South Carolina Public Service (Monks Corner)
  (803) 761-7084

South Dakota

Cities

Rapid City
 (605) 394-5329

Sioux Falls
 (800) 456-2605 (Within South Dakota)

State

State of South Dakota (Pierre)
 (605) 773-3306

Federal

Ellsworth Air Force Base (Rapid City)
 (605) 385-2485

Medical/Hospitals

Rapid City Regional Hospital (Rapid City)
 (605) 341-8375

Miscellaneous

Gateway 2000 (North Sioux City)
 (605) 232-2222

Mountain Plains Library Association (Statewide)
 (605) 677-5757

Tennessee

Cities

Knoxville
 (615) 521-2562

Memphis
 (901) 576-6548

Nashville
 (615) 862-6660

Counties

Shelby (Memphis)
 (901) 576-4434

Federal

United States Internal Revenue Service (Memphis)
 (901) 365-5656

United States Postal Service (Memphis)
 (901) 521-2336   Ext. 801

Banks

Boatmen's Bank of Tennessee (Memphis)
 (901) 762-6243

Dominion Bank (Nashville)
 (615) 251-9238

Tennesee

First American Bank (Nashville)
(615) 781-7400

First American National Bank (Memphis)
(901) 684-3264

First Tennessee Bank (Memphis)
(901) 523-5056

Leader Federal Bank for Savings (Memphis)
(901) 578-2125

National Bank of Commerce (Memphis)
(901) 523-3154

Nationsbank (Nashville)
(615) 749-3900

Union Planter's Bank (Memphis)
(901) 523-5090

Education

Memphis City Schools (Memphis)
(901) 325-5349

University of Tennessee (Knoxville)
(615) 974-6644 (Secretarial/Clerical)

University of Tennessee (Knoxville)
(615) 974-1911 (Service/Craft/Technical)

University of Tennessee (Memphis)
(901) 528-5300

Vanderbilt University (Nashville)
(615) 322-8383

Medical/Hospitals

Baptist Memorial Health Care System (Memphis)
(901) 227-4515

Baptist Memorial Hospital (Memphis)
(901) 576-6548

Centennial Medical Center (Nashville)
(615) 342-1840

Donelson Hospital (Nashville)
(615) 871-3566

Fort Sanders Regional Medical Center (Knoxville)
(615) 541-1217

Le Bonheur Children's Hospital (Memphis)
(901) 522-3164

Methodist Health Systems (Memphis)
(901) 726-8395

Miller Medical Group (Nashville)
(615) 248-7052

Regional Medical Center (Memphis)
(901) 575-8432

St. Joseph Hospital (Memphis)
(901) 577-3903

St. Jude Children's Research Hospital (Memphis)
(901) 531-2320

St. Thomas Hospital (Nashville)
(615) 386-2133

Southern Hills Medical Center (Nashville)
(615) 781-4132

Miscellaneous

American Telephone & Telegraph (Statewide)
(800) 562-7288

Tennesee

American Telephone & Telegraph (Statewide)
(800) 562-7665 (TDD)

Federal Express Corporation (Memphis)
(901) 535-9555 (Hub)

Federal Express Corporation (Memphis)
(901) 397-4260 (Office)

International Paper Company (Memphis)
(901) 763-7235

J. C. Bradford and Company (Nashville)
(615) 271-1331

Kimberly-Clark Corporation (Memphis)
(901) 529-3832

Knoxville Utilities Board (Knoxville)
(615) 558-2420

Memphis Commercial Appeal (Memphis)
(901) 529-2632

Memphis Light, Gas, and Water Company (Memphis)
(901) 528-4241

Memphis/Shelby County Public Library (Memphis)
(901) 725-8857   Ext. 1

Nashville Tennessean (Nashville)
(615) 742-7515

NIKE (Memphis)
(901) 757-6318

Nissan Motor Manufacturing Corporation (Smyrna)
(615) 355-2243

Orgill Brothers and Company (Memphis)
(901) 775-7101

Provident Life and Accident Insurance Company
(Chattanooga)
(615) 755-8507

Sharp Manufacturing of America (Memphis)
(901) 362-8772

South Central Bell Telephone Company (Memphis)
(901) 726-6560

Taco Bell (Chattanooga)
(615) 894-7011

Willis Corroon (Nashville)
(615) 872-6343

Texas

Cities

Addison
 (214) 450-2815

Amarillo
 (806) 378-4205

Arlington
 (817) 265-7938

Austin
 (512) 499-3203 (Clerical)

Austin
 (512) 499-3205 (Hospital/Healthcare)

Austin
 (512) 499-3202 (Professional)

Austin
 (512) 499-3204 (Technical/Maintenance)

Beaumont
 (409) 838-5627

Carrollton
 (214) 466-3376

Corpus Christi
 (512) 880-3333

Dallas
 (214) 670-5908

Denton
 (817) 566-8347

El Paso
 (915) 541-4094

Fort Worth
 (817) 871-7760 (General)

Fort Worth
 (817) 871-6220 (Bus Service)

Garland
 (214) 205-2349

Grand Prairie
 (214) 660-8190

Houston
 (713) 658-3798 (Clerical)

Houston
 (713) 658-3799 (Professional)

Huntsville
 (409) 291-5466

Irving
 (214) 721-2351

Lewisville
 (214) 219-3454

Lubbock
 (806) 762-2444

McKinney
 (214) 542-2675   Ext. 355

Mesquite
 (214) 216-6484

Texas

Midland
(915) 685-7245

Plainview
(806) 296-1115

Plano
(214) 578-7116

Richardson
(214) 238-4151

San Antonio
(210) 299-7280

University Park
(214) 653-3175

Counties

Bexar (San Antonio)
(210) 270-6333

Harris (Houston)
(713) 755-5044

Tarrant (Fort Worth)
(817) 884-1890

Tarrant (Fort Worth)
(817) 884-3260 (TDD)

Travis (Austin)
(512) 473-9675

State

Bureau of Prisons (El Paso)
(915) 886-4308

General Services Commission (Austin)
(512) 463-3435

Lower Colorado River Authority (San Antonio)
(512) 473-4075

Lubbock State School (Lubbock)
(806) 742-8196

Rehabilitation Commission (Austin)
(512) 483-4880

State Auditor (Austin)
(512) 479-3055

Texas Department of Human Services (Austin)
(512) 463-4700

Texas Department of Human Services (El Paso)
(915) 599-3635

Texas Department of Human Services (Odessa)
(915) 368-2413

Texas Department of Human Services (San Antonio)
(210) 337-3234

Texas Department of Insurance (Austin)
(512) 463-6170

Texas Employment Commission (Nacogdoches)
(409) 560-5193

Texas Higher Education Coordinating Board (Austin)
(512) 483-6574

Texas Water Commission (Austin)
(512) 463-7840

Travis State School (Austin)
(512) 929-6630

Federal

Brooks Air Force Base (San Antonio)
(210) 536-3810

Federal Aviation Administration (Fort Worth)
(817) 624-5855

Federal Job Information Center (Dallas)
(214) 767-8035

Federal Reserve Bank of Dallas (Dallas)
(214) 922-6166

Fort Bliss (El Paso)
(915) 568-4755

Fort Hood (Killeen)
(817) 288-2088

Internal Revenue Service (Austin)
(512) 477-5627

NASA (Houston)
(713) 483-2135

Randolph Air Force Base (San Antonio)
(210) 652-4886

Red River Army Depot (Texarkana)
(903) 334-2700

Reese Air Force Base (Lubbock)
(806) 885-6200

United States Postal Service (Austin)
(512) 929-1139

United States Postal Service (Dallas)
(214) 760-4531

United States Postal Service (Lubbock)
(806) 762-7804

United States Postal Service (San Antonio)
(210) 657-8400

United States Postal Service (Waco)
(817) 757-6536

Banks

Banc Plus Mortgage Company (San Antonio)
(210) 535-7728

Bank One of Texas (Austin)
(512) 479-5884/5805

Bank One of Texas (Dallas)
(214) 290-3637

Bank One of Texas (Fort Worth)
(817) 884-6709

Bank One of Texas (San Antonio)
(210) 657-8400

Bank United (Dallas)
(214) 404-2200

Broadway Bancshares (San Antonio)
(210) 283-6501

First City Texas (Dallas)
(214) 841-3249

First City Texas (Houston)
(713) 658-6327

First Interstate Bancorp of Texas (Houston)
(713) 250-7356

First Interstate Bank (Dallas)
  (214) 841-3249

Frost Bank (San Antonio)
  (210) 220-5627

Guaranty Fidelity Bank (Dallas)
  (214) 360-2750

Nationsbank (Austin)
  (512) 397-2495

Nationsbank (Dallas)
  (214) 712-2103

Nationsbank (San Antonio)
  (210) 270-5614

San Antonio Savings (San Antonio)
  (210) 525-5530

Team Bank (Fort Worth)
  (817) 884-6709

Texas Commerce Bancshares Incorporated (Houston)
  (713) 236-4541

Education

Alamo Community Colleges District (San Antonio)
  (210) 220-1600

Austin Community College (Austin)
  (512) 483-7648

Baylor University (Waco)
  (817) 755-3675

College of the Mainland (Houston)
  (713) 280-3991   Ext. 597

Collin County Community College (Dallas)
(214) 881-JOBS

Corpus Christi Independent School District (Corpus Christi)
(512) 886-9000

Del Mar College (Corpus Christi)
(512) 886-1190

Fort Worth Independent School District (Fort Worth)
(817) 871-2213

Houston Community College System (Houston)
(713) 866-8369 (Clerical)

Houston Community College System (Houston)
(713) 868-0711 (Professional/Technical)

McLennen Community College (Waco)
(817) 750-3612

Rice University (Houston)
(713) 527-6080

Southwest Texas State University (San Marcos)
(512) 245-2619

Stephen F. Austin University (Nacogdoches)
(409) 568-3003

Tarrant County Community College (Fort Worth)
(817) 335-6721

Texas A&M University (College Station)
(409) 845-4444

Texas Christian University (Fort Worth)
(817) 921-7791

Texas Tech University (Lubbock)
(806) 742-2211

Trinity University (San Antonio)
  (210) 736-7510

University of Texas (Arlington)
  (817) 273-3455

University of Texas (Austin)
  (512) 471-4295

University of Texas (Dallas)
  (214) 690-2400

University of Texas (Houston)
  (713) 792-4250

University of Texas (San Antonio)
  (210) 691-4650

University of Texas Health Science Center (San Antonio)
  (210) 567-2615

Hotels

Adams Mark (Houston)
  (713) 735-2700

Clarion Hotel (Dallas)
  (214) 630-7000   Ext. 7199

Doubletree Hotel (Austin)
  (512) 454-4107

Doubletree Hotel (Dallas)
  (214) 701-5279 (Lincoln Center)

Doubletree Hotel (Houston)
  (713) 968-1318 (Post Oaks)

Fairmont Hotel (Dallas)
  (214) 720-5311

Four Seasons Hotel (Houston)
  (713) 650-3437

Hilton Reservation Service (Dallas)
  (214) 770-6126

Holiday Inn (Houston)
  (713) 961-7272   Ext. 2675 (Crown Plaza)

Holiday Inn (Houston)
  (713) 558-5580   Ext. 5580 (West)

Hotel Sobitel (Houston)
  (713) 445-2082

Hyatt Regency Hotel (Dallas)
  (214) 615-6809

Hyatt Regency Hotel (Houston)
  (713) 646-6912

Hyatt Regency Hotel (San Antonio)
  (210) 222-1234   Ext. 2396

Loew's Anatole Hotel (Dallas)
  (214) 761-7333

Mansion on Turtle Creek (Dallas)
  (214) 522-2964

Marriott Hotel (Houston)
  (713) 796-2208 (Medical Center)

Marriott Hotel (Houston)
  (713) 558-8338   Ext. 1009 (Westside)

Marriott Hotel (San Antonio)
  (210) 554-6289 (River Center)

Omni Hotels (Houston)
  (713) 871-8181   Ext. 1274

Plaza Hilton (Houston)
  (713) 523-7045

Radisson Plaza Hotel (Fort Worth)
  (817) 882-1362

Richardson Hilton (Richardson)
  (214) 644-4000

Sheraton Hotel (Dallas)
  (214) 929-3103 (Grand)

Sheraton Hotel (Houston)
  (713) 442-5100   Ext. 1710 (Crown)

Stouffers (Dallas)
  (214) 631-2222

Wyndham Hotel Greensport (Houston)
  (713) 875-4506

Medical/Hospitals

Alcon Laboratories (Fort Worth)
  (817) 551-4575

All Saints Hospital (Fort Worth)
  (817) 927-6283

Arlington Memorial Hospital (Arlington)
  (817) 265-5581   Ext. 6546

Austin Diagnostic Clinic (Austin)
  (512) 453-7233

Austin Regional Clinic (Austin)
  (512) 338-5401

Austin Travis County Mental Health Center (Austin)
  (512) 440-4073

Baptist Memorial Hospital (San Antonio)
(210) 554-2099

Belle Park Hospital (Houston)
(713) 983-3420

Blue Cross/Blue Shield (Statewide)
(214) 669-5364

Brackenridge Hospital (Austin)
(512) 499-3205

Cedar Creek Hospital (Amarillo)
(806) 354-7568

Children's Medical Center (Dallas)
(214) 640-2895

Children's Medical Center (Fort Worth)
(817) 885-4414

Columbia Medical Center—East (El Paso)
(915) 595-9237

Cypress Fairbanks Medical Center (Houston)
(713) 897-3530

Doctor's Regional Medical Hospital (Corpus Christi)
(512) 857-1567

Driscoll Children's Hospital (Corpus Christi)
(512) 850-5004

Gulf Coast Regional Blood Center (Houston)
(713) 791-6666

Harris Methodist Hospital (Bedford)
(214) 933-5996

HCA Arlington Medical Center (Arlington)
(817) 347-5793

Texas

HCA Center For Health Excellence (Houston)
(713) 790-8706

HCA Denton Community Hospital (Denton)
(817) 898-7002

HCA Medical Center (Plano)
(214) 896-5300

HCA Medical Center Austin South (Austin)
(512) 338-7124

HCA Medical Center Austin South (Austin)
(800) 735-2988 (TDD)

HCA North Hills Medical Center (Fort Worth)
(817) 284-1431   Ext. 1284

Health Care Rehabilitation Center (Austin)
(512) 444-4707

Heights Hospital (Houston)
(713) 864-7103

Hendrick Medical Center (Abilene)
(915) 670-3300

High Plains Baptist Hospital (Amarillo)
(806) 358-5299

Houston NorthWest Medical Center (Houston)
(713) 440-2190 (Nonnursing)

Houston NorthWest Medical Center (Houston)
(713) 440-6321 (Nursing)

Huguley Memorial Medical Center (Fort Worth)
(817) 347-6151

Humana Hospital (Corpus Christi)
(512) 857-1567

Humana Hospital (San Antonio)
(210) 617-1700

Huntsville Memorial Hospital (Huntsville)
(409) 291-4216

Irving Health Care System (Irving)
(214) 579-8750

Johnson and Johnson Medical Inc. (Fort Worth)
(817) 784-4800

Kaiser Permanente (Dallas)
(214) 458-5138

Katy Medical Center (Houston)
(713) 395-7663

Life Management Center (El Paso)
(915) 592-6505

Lubbock Regional Mental Health Center (Lubbock)
(806) 766-0210

Memorial City Medical Center (Houston)
(713) 932-3054

Mental Health Authority of Harris County (Houston)
(713) 661-HIRE

Methodist Hospital (San Antonio)
(210) 692-4562

North East Medical Center (Houston)
(713) 540-7859

North Texas Medical Center (Dallas)
(214) 443-3301

Northwest Texas Hospital (Amarillo)
(806) 354-1905

Texas

Nueces County Mental Health Center (Corpus Christi)
(512) 886-6918

Osteopathic Medical Center of Texas (Fort Worth)
(817) 735-6524

Parkland Hospital (Dallas)
(214) 590-4473

Presbyterian Hospital (Dallas)
(214) 345-7863

Richardson Medical Center (Richardson)
(214) 680-4875

Rosewood Medical Center (Houston)
(713) 780-5812

Round Rock Hospital (Austin)
(512) 388-6400

St. Anthony's Hospital (Amarillo)
(806) 378-5087

St. David's Health Care System (Austin)
(512) 370-4369 (General)

St. David's Health Care System (Austin)
(512) 397-4000 (Nursing)

St. Joseph's Hospital (Fort Worth)
(817) 347-1420

St. Joseph's Hospital (Houston)
(713) 757-7433

St. Luke's Episcopal Hospital (Houston)
(713) 791-4131   Ext. 1

St. Mary's of the Plains Hospital (Lubbock)
(806) 796-6899

St. Paul's Medical Center (Dallas)
(214) 879-3100

Sam Houston Memorial Hospital (Houston)
(713) 932-5653

Santa Rosa Medical Center (San Antonio)
(210) 228-2343

Seton Home Care (Austin)
(512) 323-1887

Seton Medical Center (Austin)
(512) 323-1679

Shannon Medical Center (San Angelo)
(915) 657-5298

Shoal Creek Hospital (Austin)
(512) 371-6501

Sierra Medical Center (El Paso)
(915) 747-2636

Southwest General Hospital (San Antonio)
(210) 921-3439

Spohn Hospital (Corpus Christi)
(512) 881-3135

Spring Shadows Glen (Houston)
(713) 744-1615

Sun Towers Hospital (El Paso)
(915) 521-1101

Sun Towers Hospital (El Paso)
(915) 521-1102 (May contain same information found in previous entry)

Texas Tech Health Sciences Center (El Paso)
(915) 545-6523

Texas

Thomason Hospital (El Paso)
(915) 521-7960

Tomball Regional Medical Center (Tomball)
(713) 351-3739

University of Texas Southwest Medical Center (Dallas)
(214) 688-JOBS

West Houston Medical Center (Houston)
(713) 558-6734

Wichita Falls General Hospital (Wichita Falls)
(817) 761-8384

Zale Lipshy University Hospital (Dallas)
(214) 590-3484

Miscellaneous

ADVO Production (Houston)
(713) 636-7230

Allied Chemical Laboratories (Fort Worth)
(817) 268-5959   Ext. 6

American Airlines (Dallas)
(214) 425-5141

American Airlines (Fort Worth)
(817) 963-1100

American General Life (Houston)
(713) 831-3100

American Petrofina, Inc. (Dallas)
(214) 706-4258

American Statesman (Austin)
(512) 445-3706

American Telephone & Telegraph (Regional)
(800) 562-7288

American Telephone & Telegraph (Regional)
(800) 562-7665 (TDD)

Bausch and Lomb (San Antonio)
(210) 431-6300

Burns Security (Dallas)
(214) 263-2284

Caller Times (Corpus Christi)
(512) 886-3700

Capitol Metro (Austin)
(512) 389-7450

CDI (Austin)
(512) 834-6441

Central Power and Light Company (Corpus Christi)
(512) 881-5606

Central and Southwest Services (Dallas)
(214) 922-1877

Club Corporation of America (Dallas)
(214) 888-7599

Coca-Cola Bottling Company of the Southwest
(San Antonio)
(210) 229-0485

Continental Airlines (Houston)
(713) 834-5300

CSC Credit Services (Houston)
(713) 878-1920

Dalfort Aviation (Dallas)
(214) 358-7432

Texas

Dallas/Fort Worth International Airport
(214) 574-8024

El Paso Electric Company (El Paso)
(915) 543-2233

El Paso Electric Company (El Paso)
(915) 521-4720 (TDD)

Enron Corporation (Houston)
(713) 853-5884

Entex, Inc. (Houston)
(713) 657-5855

Excel (Dallas)
(214) 705-5513

Fidelity Investments (Dallas)
(214) 830-6622

Fidelity Union Life Insurance (Dallas)
(214) 978-7004

Fiesta Texas (San Antonio)
(210) 697-5000

General Laborers (Austin)
(512) 328-6692

Goodwill Industries (Austin)
(512) 478-0890

Gulf States Utilities Company (Beaumont)
(409) 839-2846

HEB Grocery Company (San Antonio)
(210) 662-5222

HEC (Dallas)
(214) 905-4780

Hoechst-Celanese (Bishop)
(512) 584-6195

Houston Cellular Telephone Company (Houston)
(713) 822-2222

Houston Instrument (Austin)
(512) 873-1525

Houston Light and Power Company (Houston)
(713) 623-3962 (Clerical)

Houston Light and Power Company (Houston)
(713) 623-3961 (Professional)

Houston Light and Power Company (Houston)
(713) 623-3963 (Semiskilled)

ICH Companies (Dallas)
(214) 954-7468

J. C. Penney Company, Inc. (Dallas)
(214) 431-2300

JDA Personnel Services (Houston)
(713) 587-6931

Lockheed Corporation (Fort Worth)
(817) 777-1000

MCI—Multi-National ACCTS (Richardson)
(800) 234-JOBS

Mary Kay Cosmetics (Dallas)
(214) 905-5266 (Corporate)

Mary Kay Cosmetics (Dallas)
(214) 905-5980 (Distributors)

Mary Kay Cosmetics (Dallas)
(214) 905-6407 (Manufacturing)

Texas

Metro Transit Authority (Richmond)
(713) 739-4089

Miller Brewing Company (Fort Worth)
(817) 551-3350

Neiman-Marcus (Dallas)
(214) 401-6975

Penzoil Company (Houston)
(713) 546-6630

Pier One Imports (Fort Worth)
(817) 878-8888

Quik Trip (Wichita Falls)
(800) 324-0935

Repcon, Inc. (Corpus Christi)
(512) 289-0909

Rohm Company (Austin)
(512) 990-6100

Rohm Company (Austin)
(512) 990-6390 (TDD)

S&A Restaurants (Dallas)
(214) 404-5622

Sea-Land (Dallas)
(214) 702-2500

Sea World of Texas (San Antonio)
(210) 523-3198

Smithkline Beecham (Dallas)
(214) 637-7219

Source, Inc. (Dallas)
(214) 851-5570

Southland Corporation (Dallas)
(214) 841-6758

Southwest Airlines (Dallas)
(214) 904-4803

Southwestern Bell Telephone (Dallas)
(214) 464-3171

Southwestern Bell Telephone (Plainview)
(806) 741-6334

Southwestern Bell Telephone (San Antonio)
(210) 820-6832

Spectradyne, Inc. (Dallas)
(214) 301-9183

Stanley Smith Security (San Antonio)
(210) 340-2305

Superior (Houston)
(713) 956-0282

Tandy Corporation (Fort Worth)
(817) 390-2949

Teanol, Inc. (North Richland Hills)
(817) 577-6429

Temple-Inland Mortgage Corporation (Austin)
(512) 469-6701

Texas Guaranteed Student Loan Corporation (Austin)
(512) 873-2999

Texas Guaranteed Student Loan Corporation (Austin)
(512) 873-2960 (TDD)

Texas Instruments (Dallas)
(214) 995-6666

Texas

Texas State Library Association (Statewide listing)
(512) 463-5470

Thrifty Car Rental (Houston)
(713) 985-5841

Tom Thumb Groceries/Drugs (Dallas)
(214) 419-7064

Tracor, Inc., Aerospace Group (Austin)
(512) 929-2100

United Service Automobile Association (San Antonio)
(210) 498-1289

Utility Engineering Corporation (Amarillo)
(806) 378-2590

Via Metropolitan Transit (San Antonio)
(210) 270-0299

Visual Numerics (Houston)
(713) 242-6690

Word Temps (Dallas)
(214) 419-1733

Workforce Development Corporation (Corpus Christi)
(512) 854-5627

Zale Corporation (Dallas)
(214) 580-5408

Utah

Cities

Murray
 (801) 264-2525

Orem
 (801) 224-7170

Provo
 (801) 379-6187

Salt Lake City
 (801) 535-6625

Counties

Davis (Farmington)
 (801) 451-3484

Salt Lake (Salt Lake City)
 (801) 468-2390

Salt Lake (Salt Lake City)
 (801) 468-3600 (TDD)

Utah (Provo)
 (801) 370-8585

Weber (Ogden)
 (801) 399-8409

Utah

State

Utah State Veterans Job Hotline (Statewide)
(801) 269-4775

Federal

Federal Job Information Center (Statewide)
(800) 359-3997 (Press 1)

Federal Job Information Center (Statewide)
(800) 326-2996 (TDD)

Federal Job Opportunities (Statewide)
(303) 969-7053

Hill Air Force Base (Hillfield)
(801) 777-3762

Banks

First Security Bank of Utah (Salt Lake)
(801) 246-1885 (Bank)

First Security Bank of Utah (Salt Lake)
(801) 246-1850 (Bank/Rotary Telephone)

First Security Bank of Utah (Salt Lake)
(801) 246-6440 (Operations Center)

First Security Bank of Utah (Salt Lake)
(801) 426-6310 (Operations Center/Rotary Telephone)

Key Bank (Salt Lake City)
(801) 535-1117

West One Bank (Salt Lake City)
(801) 537-6994

Education

Alpine School District (Alpine)
  (801) 756-8462

Brigham Young University (Provo)
  (801) 378-4357

Salt Lake Community College (Redwood Campus)
  (801) 967-4133

University of Utah (Salt Lake City)
  (801) 581-JOBS

Utah Valley Community College (Orem)
  (801) 222-8000   Ext. 8185

Medical/Hospitals

Alta View Hospital (Sandy)
  (801) 576-2698

Cottonwood Hospital Medical Center (Orem)
  (801) 269-2750

FHP Health Care (Orem)
  (801) 355-1422

Holy Cross/Jordan Valley Hospital (Orem)
  (801) 350-4020

IHC Hospital of Utah County (Orem)
  (801) 371-7036

Intermountain Healthcare Inc. (Salt Lake City)
  (801) 533-3754

LDS Hospital (Salt Lake City)
  (801) 321-1333

Mountain View Hospital (Payson)
  (801) 465-7141

Utah

Murdock Healthcare (Springville)
(801) 489-1501

Pioneer Valley Hospital (West Valley City)
(801) 964-3562

Primary Children's Medical Center (Salt Lake City)
(801) 588-2200

University Hospital (Salt Lake City)
(801) 581-2310

University of Utah Medical Center (Salt Lake City)
(801) 581-2300

Miscellaneous

American Telephone & Telegraph (Salt Lake City)
(801) 269-3220

American Telephone & Telegraph (Salt Lake City)
(801) 269-3267 (TDD)

Bonneville International Corporation (Salt Lake City)
(801) 575-7511

Cellular One of Utah (Salt Lake City)
(801) 580-7815

Church of Jesus Christ of Latter Day Saints (Statewide)
(801) 240-2018

Discover Card (Sandy)
(801) 565-5525

Discover Card (Sandy)
(801) 565-5675 (TDD)

Eaton Kenway (Salt Lake City)
(801) 530-4688

Fred Meyer, Inc. (Salt Lake City)
(800) 401-JOBS

KUTV Channel 2 NBC (Salt Lake City)
(801) 973-5425

Morris Air Service (Salt Lake City)
(801) 483-6508

Mountain Fuel (Salt Lake City)
(801) 534-5100

Mountain Plains Library Association (Statewide)
(605) 677-5757

Novell Incorporated (Provo)
(801) 429-5390

Nu-Skin International (Salt Lake City)
(801) 345-2525

Pacificorp (Salt Lake City)
(801) 220-2974

Valtek Inc. (Springville)
(801) 489-2220

WordPerfect Corporation (Orem)
(801) 222-7600

Vermont

Cities

Burlington
  (802) 865-7157

State

Vermont State Jobline (Montpelier)
  (802) 828-3484

Education

St. Michael's College (Colchester)
  (802) 654-3200

University of Vermont (Burlington)
  (802) 656-2248

Medical/Hospitals

Medical Center Hospital of Vermont (Burlington)
  (801) 656-2722

University Health Center (Burlington)
  (802) 656-8029

Miscellaneous

American Telephone & Telegraph (Statewide)
  (800) 858-5417

New England Library Association (Statewide)
  (617) 738-3148

Virginia

Cities

Alexandria
(703) 838-4422 (General)

Alexandria
(703) 739-8360 (Metropolitan Washington Airports Authority)

Chesapeake
(804) 547-6416

Fairfax
(703) 385-7860

Falls Church
(703) 241-5163

Hampton
(804) 727-6406

Lynchburg
(804) 847-1346

Newport News
(804) 928-9281

Norfolk
(804) 627-8768

Petersburg
(804) 796-9991

Portsmouth
(804) 398-0682

Virginia

Richmond
 (804) 780-5888 (General)

Richmond
 (804) 751-5957 (Metropolitan Authority)

Roanoke
 (703) 981-2099

Suffolk
 (804) 925-6435

Virginia Beach
 (804) 427-3580   Ext. 788

Counties

Arlington (Arlington)
 (703) 538-3363

Fairfax (Fairfax)
 (703) 324-5627

James City (Williamsburg)
 (804) 253-6736

Loudoun (Leesburg)
 (703) 777-5036

Prince William (Manassas)
 (703) 792-6645   Ext. 332

State

Department of General Services (Richmond)
 (804) 786-3055

Department of General Services (Richmond)
 (804) 786-6152 (TDD)

Department of Rehabilitative Service (Richmond)
 (804) 278-0745

Department of Rehabilitative Service (Richmond)
(804) 367-0236 (TDD)

Department of Transportation (Fairfax)
(703) 912-4093

Department of Transportation (Richmond)
(804) 278-0234

Maryland National Capitol Park and Planning Commission (McLean)
(703) 538-3361

Federal

Defense Intelligence Agency (Arlington)
(703) 284-1110

Department of the Air Force (Arlington)
(703) 693-6550

Department of the Army (Arlington)
(703) 693-7911

Department of Commerce—Patent and Trademark Office (Arlington)
(703) 305-4221

Freddi Mac (McLean)
(703) 903-2970

Langley Air Force Base (Hampton)
(804) 764-4892

National Technical Information Service (Fairfax)
(703) 487-4680 Ext. 1

National Weather Service (Norfolk)
(804) 441-3720

Norfolk Naval Shipyard (Portsmouth)
(804) 396-5657

Virginia

Norfolk Navy Base (Norfolk)
(804) 444-7541

Norfolk Navy Base (Norfolk)
(804) 444-7542 (Rotary Telephone)

Office of Personnel Management (Norfolk)
(804) 441-3355

Peninsula Civilian Personnel Support Activities
(Norfolk)
(804) 873-3160   Ext. 400

United States Army Civilian Personnel Center
(Alexandria)
(703) 325-8841

United States Central Intelligence Agency (Langley)
(703) 351-2028

United States Defense Information System Agency
(Arlington)
(703) 746-1724

United States Defense Nuclear Agency (Alexandria)
(703) 325-0138

United States Fish and Wildlife Service (Arlington)
(703) 358-2120

United States Forest Service (Alexandria)
(703) 235-JOBS

United States Geologic Survey (Reston)
(703) 648-7676

United States Marine Corps Headquarters (Arlington)
(703) 697-7474

United States Minerals Management Service (Herndon)
(703) 787-1402

United States Naval Surface Warfare Center (Dahlgren)
(703) 663-8067

United States Postal Service (Norfolk)
(804) 629-2225

Banks

Ameribanc Savings Bank (Falls Church)
(703) 658-5627

Central Fidelity Bank, Inc. (Lynchburg)
(804) 847-9231

Central Fidelity Bank, Inc. (Richmond)
(804) 697-7193

Central Fidelity Bank, Inc. (Roanoke)
(703) 983-8288

Crestar Bank (Richmond)
(804) 270-8572

Dominion Bank (Roanoke)
(703) 563-7907

First American Bank (Fairfax)
(703) 760-6875

First American Bank (McLean)
(703) 903-7770

Nationsbank (Norfolk)
(804) 441-4451

Pentagon Federal Credit Union (Arlington)
(703) 838-1200   Ext. 1

Signet Bank (Falls Church)
(703) 827-6007

Virginia

Education

Alexandria Public Schools (Alexandria)
(703) 824-6624

Fairfax County Schools (Fairfax)
(703) 750-8569 (Education/Management)

Fairfax County Schools (Fairfax)
(703) 750-8533 (Support)

Fairfax County Schools (Fairfax)
(703) 750-8400 (Teaching)

George Mason University (Fairfax)
(703) 993-8799

Hampton-Newport News School Board (Hampton)
(804) 826-8015

Medical College of Hampton Road (Norfolk)
(804) 446-5700

Norfolk State University (Norfolk)
(804) 683-8184

Northern Virginia Community College (Fairfax)
(703) 323-3444

Northern Virginia Training Center (Fairfax)
(703) 323-2804

Old Dominion University (Norfolk)
(804) 683-4011 (Administrative, Professional, Science, Trades)

Old Dominion University (Norfolk)
(804) 683-3066 (Clerical)

Prince William County Public Schools (Manassas)
(703) 791-2776

Radford University (Radford)
(703) 831-5825

University of Virginia (Charlottesville)
(804) 924-4400 (Administrative/Technical/Professional)

University of Virginia (Charlottesville)
(804) 924-4411 (Secretarial/Clerical)

Virginia State University (Petersburg)
(804) 524-JOBS

Hotels

Hyatt Regency (Crystal City)
(703) 418-7228

Marriott Corporation (Alexandria)
(703) 461-6100

Marriott Corporation (Alexandria)
(703) 461-6115 (Spanish)

McLean Hilton (McLean)
(703) 761-5155

Radisson Plaza Hotel (Alexandria)
(703) 671-2483

Ramada Tysons Corner (Falls Church)
(703) 821-3161

Medical/Hospitals

American Medical Laboratories (Chantilly)
(703) 802-7282

American Red Cross—Tidewater Chapter (Norfolk)
(804) 446-7293

Virginia

Blue Cross/Blue Shield of Virginia (Richmond)
(804) 354-5627

Children's Hospital (Norfolk)
(804) 640-0071

Fairfax Hospital (Falls Church)
(703) 698-2374

HCA Reston Hospital Center (Reston)
(703) 481-9063

Holy Cross Hospital (Falls Church)
(703) 538-2235

Humana Hospital, Bayside (Portsmouth)
(804) 363-6608

Kaiser Permanente (Norfolk)
(800) 326-4005

Kimberly Quality Care (Richmond)
(804) 388-3222

Loudoun Hospital Center (Leesburg)
(703) 779-5424

Maryview Medical Center (Portsmouth)
(804) 398-2240

Medical College of Virginia Hospital (Richmond)
(804) 278-0266

Mount Vernon Hospital (Alexandria)
(703) 664-7258

Obici Hospital (Suffolk)
(804) 934-4473

Opima Health Plans (Norfolk)
(804) 552-7200

Portsmouth General Hospital (Portsmouth)
(804) 398-4559

Portsmouth General Hospital (Portsmouth)
(804) 398-4909 (May contain same information found in previous entry)

Potomac Hospital (Alexandria)
(703) 670-1836

Sentara Bayside Hospital (Virginia Beach)
(804) 363-6608

Sentara General Hospital (Norfolk)
(804) 628-3717

Sentara Leigh Hospital (Norfolk)
(804) 466-6659

Tidewater Health Care (Virginia Beach)
(804) 481-8668

Veterans Administration Medical Center (Hampton)
(804) 722-3107

Virginia Beach General Hospital (Virginia Beach)
(804) 481-8668

Miscellaneous

American Automobile Association (Fairfax)
(703) 222-5627   Ext. 2

American Telephone & Telegraph (Statewide)
(800) 562-7288

American Telephone & Telegraph (Statewide)
(800) 562-7665 (TDD)

American Tobacco Company (Chester)
(804) 751-2828

Virginia

Bell Atlantic Network Services (Falls Church)
(703) 204-7201

Caci International, Inc. (Alexandria)
(703) 841-8802

Christian Broadcasting Network (Richmond)
(804) 523-7363

Circuit City (Richmond)
(804) 527-4094

Colonial Williamsburg (Williamsburg)
(804) 220-7129

District of Columbia Natural Gas (Fairfax)
(703) 750-5817

Gannett Company Inc. (Arlington)
(703) 284-6054

General Electric Corporation (Alexandria)
(703) 665-3357

General Research Corporation (Vienna)
(703) 506-5129

Giant Food (Vienna)
(703) 425-4820

GTE (Chantilly)
(703) 818-5627

International Business Machines (Manassas)
(703) 367-0728

Labat-Anderson (Arlington)
(703) 523-9400   Ext. 250

Lendmen (Norfolk)
(804) 473-2980   Ext. 9951

McDonald's Corporation (McLean)
(703) 698-4001

MCI (Alexandria)
(703) 486-6420

Media General Cable (Fairfax)
(703) 738-3440

Meridian Corporation (Alexandria)
(703) 998-3635

Metro Network (Falls Church)
(703) 893-8931

Mobil Oil Corporation (Fairfax)
(703) 849-6005 (Marketing Jobs)

Mobil Oil Corporation (Fairfax)
(703) 846-2777 (Office/Support Staff)

Network Management, Inc. (Fairfax)
(703) 359-9400   Ext. 5627

Norfolk Shipbuilding and Drydock (Norfolk)
(804) 494-2964

Norshipco (Norfolk)
(804) 494-2964

Sprint International (Herndon)
(703) 689-7900   Ext. 1

TRW, Inc. (Fairfax)
(703) 968-2001

TV Answer, Inc. (Fairfax)
(703) 715-8826

US Air, Inc. (Alexandria)
(703) 418-7499

Virginia

Virginia Library Association (Statewide)
(703) 519-8027

Virginia Power and Electric Company (Fairfax)
(703) 359-3300

Washington Gas and Light (Fairfax)
(703) 750-5814

WETA-TV Channel 26 (Shirlington)
(703) 820-6025

Wheat First Securities Inc. (Richmond)
(804) 965-2262

Washington

Cities

Auburn
 (206) 931-3077

Bellevue
 (206) 455-7822

Bothell
 (206) 486-9473

Bremerton
 (206) 478-5241

Everett
 (206) 259-8768

Federal Way
 (206) 661-4089

Kent
 (206) 859-3375

Kirkland
 (206) 828-1161

Lacey
 (206) 491-3213

Mercer Island
 (206) 236-5323   Ext. 326

Olympia
 (206) 753-8383

Washington

Olympia
(206) 586-0545 (May contain same information found in previous entry)

Puyallup
(206) 841-5596

Redmond
(206) 556-2121

Renton
(206) 235-2514

Seattle
(206) 684-7999 (General)

Seattle
(206) 443-4376 (Housing Authority)

Seattle
(206) 684-1313 (Metro Municipality)

Seattle
(206) 728-3290   Ext. 2 (Port of Seattle)

Spokane
(509) 625-6161

Spokane
(509) 456-2889 (May contain same information found in previous entry)

Tacoma
(206) 591-5795

Tukwila
(206) 433-1828

Vancouver
(206) 696-8128

Yakima
(509) 575-6098

Counties

Clark (Vancouver)
(206) 737-6018

King (Seattle)
(206) 296-5209

Pierce (Tacoma)
(206) 591-7466

Snohomish (Everett)
(206) 388-3686

Spokane (Spokane)
(509) 328-0590

Thurston (Tumwater)
(206) 786-5499

Whatcom (Bellingham)
(206) 738-4550

State

Washington State Jobline (Olympia)
(206) 586-0545

Washington State Jobline (Seattle)
(206) 464-7378

Washington State Jobline (Spokane)
(509) 456-2889

Federal

Bangor Naval Submarine Base (Bangor)
(206) 396-4779

Washington

Bonneville Power Administration (Seattle)
(206) 553-7564

Department of Housing and Urban Development
(Seattle)
(206) 553-8141

Fairchild Air Force Base (Spokane)
(509) 247-2132

Federal Aviation Administration (Seattle)
(206) 227-1012

Federal Emergency Management Agency (Seattle)
(206) 487-4600

Fort Lewis (Fort Lewis)
(206) 967-5377

McChord Air Force Base (Seattle)
(206) 984-2277

National Oceanic and Atmospheric Administration
(Seagoing Vessels)
(206) 526-6051

National Weather Service (Seattle)
(206) 526-6294

Office of Personnel Management (Seattle)
(206) 220-6400

Office of Personnel Management (Seattle)
(206) 442-4365 (May contain same information found
in previous entry)

Puget Sound Naval Shipyard (Seattle)
(206) 476-3110

United States Army Corps of Engineers (Seattle)
(206) 764-3739

United States Department of Commerce (Seattle)
(206) 526-6294

United States Internal Revenue Service (Seattle)
(206) 220-5757

United States Postal Service (Seattle)
(206) 442-6240

United States Postal Service (Tacoma)
(206) 756-6148

Banks

Boeing Employee's Credit Union (Seattle)
(206) 439-5725

Evergreen Bank (Seattle)
(206) 628-8740

First Interstate Bank of Washington (Seattle)
(206) 292-3551

Key Bank (Tacoma)
(800) 677-6150

Key Bank (Tacoma)
(800) 688-6191 (TDD/During business hours)

Pacific First Bank (Seattle)
(206) 224-3330

Puget Sound National Bank (Tacoma)
(206) 593-5307

SeaFirst National Bank (Seattle)
(206) 358-7523

U.S. Bank of Washington (Seattle)
(206) 344-5656

Washington Mutual Federal Savings
(800) 952-0787 (Within Washington Only)

Washington Mutual Federal Savings (Seattle)
(206) 461-8787

Education

Bates Technical Colleges (Tacoma)
(206) 596-1652

Battle Ground Public Schools (Seattle)
(206) 687-6535

Bellevue Public Schools No. 405 (Bellevue)
(206) 455-6009

Bethel School District (Seattle)
(206) 536-7270

Central Kitsap Public Schools (Spokane)
(509) 698-3475

Clover School District (Spokane)
(206) 589-7436

Everett School District No. 2 (Everett)
(206) 259-2935

Evergreen School District (Seattle)
(206) 254-7403

Evergreen State College (Tacoma)
(206) 866-6000   Ext. 6361

Federal Way Public Schools (Federal Way)
(206) 941-2058

Franklin Pierce School District (Seattle)
(206) 848-6661

Highline Community College (Seattle)
(206) 878-3710

Issaquah School District No. 411 (Issaquah)
(206) 392-0707

Kent School District (Kent)
 (206) 859-7500

Lake Washington School District No. 414 (Kirkland)
 (206) 828-3243

Marysville School District No. 25 (Marysville)
 (206) 653-0807

Mead School District No. 354 (Freya)
 (509) 468-3193

Mercer Island School District No. 400 (Mercer Island)
 (206) 236-3302

Pacific Lutheran University (Seattle)
 (206) 535-8598

Pierce College (Tacoma)
 (206) 964-7341

Puyallup School District No. 3 (Tacoma)
 (206) 841-8666

Seattle Community College (Seattle)
 (206) 587-5454

South Kitsap Public Schools (Spokane)
 (509) 876-7389

Spokane Public Schools (Spokane)
 (509) 353-7639 (Certified)

Spokane Public Schools (Spokane)
 (509) 353-5459 (Classified)

Tacoma School District (Tacoma)
 (206) 596-1300 (Certified)

Tacoma School District (Tacoma)
 (206) 596-1265 (Classified)

University of Puget Sound (Seattle)
(206) 756-3368

University of Washington (Seattle)
(206) 223-3233 (Hospital)

University of Washington (Seattle)
(206) 543-6969 (Staff)

University of Washington (Seattle)
(206) 543-1827 (Temporary Services)

Washington State University (Pullman)
(509) 335-7637

Yakima School District No. 9 (Yakima)
(509) 575-2988

Hotels

Marriott Management Service (Bellevue)
(206) 451-9477

Red Lion Hotels and Inns (Vancouver)
(503) 240-8598

Sheraton Seattle Hotel and Towers (Seattle)
(206) 287-5505

Medical/Hospitals

Associated Health Services (Tacoma)
(206) 552-1841

Auburn General Hospital (Seattle)
(206) 833-7711   Ext. 429

Blue Cross/Blue Shield of Washington and Alaska
(Mountlake Terrace)
(206) 670-4773

Children's Hospital and Medical Center (Seattle)
(206) 526-2230

Everett Clinic (Everett)
(206) 339-5400

Everett Clinic (Everett)
(800) 533-7035   Ext. 5400 (Within Washington only)

Evergreen Hospital (Seattle)
(206) 899-2502

Fred Hutchinson Cancer Research Center (Seattle)
(206) 467-2977

Good Samaritan Hospital (Seattle)
(206) 848-6661   Ext. 1905

Group Health Cooperative (Bellevue/Seattle/Tacoma)
(206) 448-2745 (Administrative)

Group Health Cooperative (Bellevue/Seattle/Tacoma)
(206) 448-2744 (LPNS)

Group Health Cooperative (Bellevue/Seattle/Tacoma)
(206) 448-2743 (Nursing)

Group Health Cooperative (Bellevue/Seattle/Tacoma)
(206) 383-7832 (South)

Group Health Northwest (Spokane)
(509) 838-3390

Harborview Medical (Seattle)
(206) 223-8409

Harrison Memorial Hospital (Bremerton)
(206) 792-6729

Highline Community Hospital (Seattle)
(206) 431-5325

Washington

King County Medical Center (Seattle)
(206) 899-2520

Laboratory of Pathology (Seattle)
(206) 386-2990

Multicare Medical Center (Tacoma)
(206) 594-1256

Northwest Hospital (Seattle)
(206) 368-1791 (Nonnursing)

Northwest Hospital (Seattle)
(206) 368-1984 (Nursing)

Northwest Kidney Center (Seattle)
(206) 292-2771   Ext. 6924

Pacific Medical Center (Seattle)
(206) 326-4120

Providence Medical Center (Everett)
(206) 258-7562

Providence Medical Center (Seattle)
(206) 320-2020

Puget Sound Blood Center (Seattle)
(206) 292-2302

Puget Sound Hospital (Seattle)
(206) 474-0561   Ext. 103

Sacred Heart Medical Center (Spokane)
(509) 455-3192

St. Clare's Hospital (Tacoma)
(206) 581-6419

St. Francis' Community Hospital (Federal Way)
(206) 927-9700   Ext. 6990

St. Francis' Community Hospital (Tacoma)
(206) 838-9700   Ext. 6990

St. Joseph's Hospital (Tacoma)
(206) 591-6623

St. Peter's Hospital (Olympia)
(206) 493-7779

Stevens Hospital (Edmonds)
(206) 744-4194

Swedish Hospital Medical Center (Seattle)
(206) 386-2888

Tacoma General Hospital Medical Center (Tacoma)
(206) 594-1256

University of Washington Medical Center (Seattle)
(206) 548-4470

Valley Medical Center (Renton)
(206) 251-5190

Virginia Mason Clinic (Seattle)
(206) 223-6496

Miscellaneous

Advanced Technology Laboratories (Seattle)
(206) 487-7799 (After 3 P.M.–Before 8 A.M.)

Airborne Express Corporation (Seattle)
(206) 281-4815

Alaska Airlines (Seattle)
(206) 433-3230

Alpac Corporation (Seattle)
(206) 326-7436

Applied Microsystems Corporation (Seattle)
(206) 882-5668

Washington

Associated Grocers (Seattle)
(206) 767-8788

Battelle Memorial Institute (Richland)
(509) 367-4056

Boeing Company (Seattle)
(206) 394-3111

Bugle and Gates (Seattle)
(206) 621-2639

Catholic Archdiocese (Seattle)
(206) 382-4564

Darigold (Seattle)
(206) 286-6730

Drug Emporium Northwest (Statewide)
(206) 646-1629

Eldec Corporation (Olympia)
(206) 743-8215

Ernst Corporation (Seattle)
(206) 621-6880

Frank Russell Company (Seattle)
(206) 595-5454

Fred Meyer Inc. (Seattle)
(800) 401-JOBS

GTE (Seattle)
(206) 261-5777 (Hourly)

GTE (Seattle)
(206) 261-5667 (Management)

Hewlett-Packard, Instrument Division (Seattle)
(206) 334-2244

Holland America Line Westours (Seattle)
(206) 286-3496

Immunek Corporation (Seattle)
(206) 389-4060

Intermec Corporation (Seattle)
(206) 348-2820

International Business Machines (Statewide)
(800) 831-2303 (within Washington only)

John Fluke Company (Seattle)
(206) 356-5205

Keiser Aluminum (Tacoma)
(206) 591-0425

Key Tronic Corporation (Spokane)
(509) 927-5209

King Broadcasting Company (Seattle)
(206) 448-3915

KIRO (Seattle)
(206) 728-5205

Manpower Temporary Service (Seattle)
(206) 447-5627

McCaw Cellular Communications (Kirkland)
(206) 828-8484

Metro Transportation (Seattle)
(206) 684-1313

Microsoft Corporation (Seattle)
(206) 936-5500

Microsoft Corporation (Seattle)
(800) 892-3181

Morning News Tribune (Tacoma)
(206) 597-8590

Washington

Pacific Telcom Inc. (Vancouver)
(206) 699-5990

Pemco Financial Center (Seattle)
(206) 628-8748

Physio-Control (Seattle)
(206) 867-4130

Pierce Transit (Olympia)
(206) 581-8097

Puget Sound Power and Light Company (Bellevue)
(206) 462-3540

Royal Seafood, Inc. (Seattle)
(206) 285-1105

Safeco Corporation (Seattle)
(206) 545-3233

Schuck's (Seattle)
(206) 448-8779

Sea-Land Service, Inc. (Seattle)
(206) 593-8042

Seattle Public Library (Seattle)
(206) 386-4120

Senior Jobs Hotline (Seattle)
(206) 684-0477

Sharp Microelectronics Technology (Camas)
(800) 874-2771

Sundstrand Data Control Inc. (Redmond)
(206) 885-8605

United Parcel Service (Seattle)
(206) 621-6329

USWEST Communications (Seattle)
 (206) 345-6126

Washington Water and Power Company (Spokane)
 (509) 482-4281

West Coast Grocers (Tacoma)
 (206) 593-5876

Windstar Line Westours (Shipboard)
 (206) 286-3496   Ext. 2

West Virginia

Federal

Office of Personnel Management (Statewide)
(513) 225-2866 Ext. 1

Office of Personnel Management (Statewide)
(513) 225-2720 (May contain same information found in previous entry)

Education

Kanawha County Board of Education (Charleston)
(304) 348-6193

Putnam County Board of Education (Winfield)
(304) 586-0555

West Virginia University (Morgantown)
(304) 293-7234

Miscellaneous

American Telephone & Telegraph (Statewide)
(800) 562-7288

American Telephone & Telegraph (Statewide)
(800) 562-7665 (TDD)

Pennsylvania Cooperative Job Hotline (Library Listings)
(717) 234-4646

Wisconsin

Cities

Madison
 (608) 266-6500

Milwaukee
 (414) 278-5555

Counties

Milwaukee (Milwaukee)
 (414) 278-5321

Federal

Federal Job Information Center (Statewide)
 (312) 353-6189

Banks

Anchor Bank (Madison)
 (608) 252-8841

Banc One Wisconsin Corporation (Milwaukee)
 (414) 765-2677

Firstar Bank (Milwaukee)
 (414) 765-JOBS

Firstar Bank (Milwaukee)
 (414) 765-5445 (TDD)

Wisconsin

First Wisconsin National Bank (Milwaukee)
(414) 765-5111

Mutual Savings Bank (Milwaukee)
(414) 362-6180

Education

Madison Area Technical College (Madison)
(608) 246-6906

Marquette University (Milwaukee)
(414) 288-7000

Milwaukee Area Technical College (Milwaukee)
(414) 278-6807

University of Wisconsin (Madison)
(414) 229-6629

Medical/Hospitals

Children's Hospital of Wisconsin (Milwaukee)
(414) 266-2732

Columbia Hospital (Milwaukee)
(414) 961-3763

Community Memorial Hospital (Menomonee Falls)
(414) 251-1002   Ext. 3046

Falls Medical Group (Menomonee Falls)
(414) 251-9601

Froedtert Memorial Lutheran Hospital (Milwaukee)
(414) 259-2040

Meriter Health Services (Madison)
(608) 267-6055

St. Joseph's Hospital (Milwaukee)
(414) 447-2157

St. Luke's Medical Center (Milwaukee)
(414) 649-6378

St. Mary's Hospital (Milwaukee)
(414) 291-1269

Miscellaneous

Goodwill Industries (Milwaukee)
(414) 273-9463 (Within Milwaukee)

Goodwill Industries (Milwaukee)
(800) 353-JOBS (Within Wisconsin)

Harley Davidson (Milwaukee)
(414) 535-3687

M&I Data Service, Inc. (Milwaukee)
(414) 357-JOBS

Marshall and Isley Corporation (Milwaukee)
(414) 765-8300

Milwaukee County Transit System (Milwaukee)
(414) 937-0471

Northwestern Mutual Life Insurance Company
(Wausau)
(414) 299-7070

Springs Window Fashions Division (Middleton)
(608) 836-5323

Wisconsin Electric and Power Company (Milwaukee)
(414) 221-3091

Wisconsin Gas Company (Milwaukee)
(414) 291-6756

Wyoming

Federal

Federal Job Opportunities Center (Statewide)
(303) 969-7052

Education

Laramie County School District (Laramie)
(307) 771-2448

University of Wyoming (Laramie)
(307) 766-5602

Medical/Hospitals

Wyoming Medical Center (Casper)
(307) 577-2593

Miscellaneous

Mountain Plains Library Association (Statewide)
(605) 677-5757

SafeCard Service (Cheyenne)
(307) 771-2761

Other Listings

National Joblines

Federal

Central Intelligence Agency
  (800) 562-7242

Federal Job College Hotline
  (900) 990-9200 (40¢ Per Minute)

National Park Service
  (202) 619-7111

United States Department of the Interior
  (800) 336-4562

United States Department of Labor
  (800) 366-2753

Hotels

Choice International Hotels/Manor Care Inc.
  (800) 348-2041

Holiday Inns
  (404) 241-7249

Medical/Hospitals

American Association for Respiratory Disease
  (214) 241-7249

Charter Medical Corporation
  (800) 334-5392

Medical Library Association
  (312) 419-9094

National Hospice Organization
  (703) 243-4348

Miscellaneous

Airline Pilot's Association
  (703) 689-4262

American Association of Botanical Gardens and Arboretors
  (215) 688-8127 (5 P.M. to 8 A.M., Mon. through Fri./24 Hours on Weekends)

American Association of Law Libraries
  (312) 939-7877

American Library Association
  (800) 545-2433 (Outside Illinois)

American Library Association
  (800) 545-2444 (Within Illinois)

American Library Association
  (312) 280-2464 (Within Area Code)

Asian American Journalist Association
  (415) 346-2261

Association of College and Research Libraries
  (312) 944-6795

California Media and Library Educators Association
  (415) 697-8832

Career America Connection
  (912) 757-3000

National Joblines

Cleveland Area Metropolitan Library Jobline
(216) 921-4702

Computer Data Systems, Inc.
(800) 772-2374

Corporation for Public Broadcasting
(202) 393-1045

Delaware Library Association
(302) 739-4748   Ext. 69

Delaware Library Association
(800) 282-8696 (Within Delaware)

Drexel University College of Information Studies
(215) 895-1672

Editorial Freelancers Association
(212) 260-6470

Employee Relocation Council
(202) 857-0842

Fred Meyer
(800) 401-JOBS

Illinois Library Association
(312) 828-0930 (Professional Staff)

Illinois Library Association
(312) 828-9198 (Support Staff)

MCI—Business Markets
(800) 274-5758

MCI—International
(800) 888-2413

MCI—Strategy and Technology
(800) 456-5243

MCI—Other Strategy and Technology
(800) 289-0128

Maryland Library Association
(410) 685-5760

Missouri Library Association
(314) 442-6590

Nature Conservancy
(703) 247-3721

New England Library Jobline
(617) 738-3148

New Jersey Library Association
(609) 695-2121

New York Library Association
(518) 432-6952

New York Library Association
(800) 232-6952 (Within New York)

Northern Telecom
(800) 667-8437) (Press 9, 8 A.M. to 5 P.M., Mon. through Fri., Eastern Time)

Oklahoma Department of Libraries
(405) 521-4202

Pennsylvania Cooperative Job Hotline
(717) 234-4646

PetsMart
(800) 899-7387   Ext. 5900

Radio-Television News Directors Association
(900) 407-8632 (75¢ Per Minute)

San Francisco Bay–San Andreas/Special Libraries Association
(415) 856-2140

Southern California Chapter, Special Libraries
  Association
  (818) 795-2145

Special Libraries Association
  (202) 234-3632

Sundt Corporation
  (800) 873-6078

Systems and Computer Technology (SCT)
  (800) 722-2344

Texas Library Association
  (512) 328-1518

United Airlines System Jobline
  (708) 952-7077

University of South Carolina College of Information
  Science
  (803) 777-8443

Virginia Library Association
  (703) 519-8027

Women in Communications
  (800) 765-9424

International Listings

Government

United States Central Intelligence Agency
(800) 562-7242

United States Office of Personnel Management (Guam)
(808) 541-2784

United States Office of Personnel Management (Guam)
(011) 671-472-7451 (May contain same information found in previous entry)

United States Office of Personnel Management
(Puerto Rico)
(809) 774-8790

United States Peace Corps (Volunteer)
(800) 424-8580

Education

University of Western Ontario School of Library and Information Science (Canada)
(519) 661-3543

Hotels

Holiday Inns International (Worldwide)
(404) 604-5627

Medical/Hospitals

St. Paul's Hospital (Vancouver, British Columbia, Canada)
 (604) 631-5243

Miscellaneous

British Columbia Library Association (Canada)
 (604) 430-6411

Servico Pacific, Inc. (Guam)
 (808) 531-5515

Mail Joblines

Miscellaneous

American Society for Information Science (National)
  ASIS Jobline
  ASIS Headquarters
  8720 Georgia Avenue
  Suite 501
  Silver Springs, MD 20910-3602

Institutional Library Mail Jobline (National)
  Rhode Island Department of State Library Service
  300 Richmond Street
  Providence, RI 02903
  Attention: S. Carlson
  (Note: Send self-addressed stamped envelope)

Iowa Library Job List (Iowa)
  State Library of Iowa
  East 12th and Grand
  Des Moines, IA 50319
  Attention: Doris Collette

Music Library Association (National)
  Business Office
  Music Library Association
  P.O. Box 487
  Canton, ME 02021
  (Note: $10 yearly subscription fee)

Mail Joblines

Rhode Island Library Association (Southeast New England)
  Government Publications Office
  University Library
  University of Rhode Island
  Kingston, RI 02881
  Attention: Pamela Stoddard
  (Note: Send self-addressed stamped envelope)

Rural Libraries Jobline (National)
  College of Library Science
  Clarion University of Pennsylvania
  Clarion, PA 16224
  Attention: Michael Jaugstetter
  (Note: Send $1 per copy)

Veterans Affairs Library Register
  Learning Resources Service (142)
  Veterans Affairs Central Office
  810 Vermont Avenue, NW
  Washington, DC 20420
  Attention: Wendy Carter

Marcia P. Williams
P.O. Box 211113
Denver, Colorado 80221

Addition:

   Company Name _____

   Jobline Telephone Number (   ) _____

   Type of Business _____

Correction:

   Company Name _____

   New Jobline Telephone Number (   ) _____

   Book Page Number_____

Remarks: _____

_____

_____

_____

_____

_____

Optional:

   Your Name _____

   Address _____

_____

Thank you for your interest in The National Job Hotline Directory.